TIM FOUNTAIN

Tim Fountain both teaches playwriting and is a playwright himself. He was Literary Manager at The Bush Theatre, London from 1997–2001, and is currently a lecturer in creative writing at Strathclyde University.

His plays include *Sex Addict* (Royal Court Theatre), *Resident Alien* (Bush Theatre and New York Theatre Workshop, Adelaide Festival Centre, OTB Seattle and UK Tour, also broadcast on BBC Radio 3), *Julie Burchill is Away*, *Hotboi* and *How to Lose Friends and Alienate People* (all at Soho Theatre), and an adaptation of *Midnight Cowboy* (Assembly Rooms, Edinburgh). He was a principal writer on the animated sitcom *Bob and Margaret* (Comedy Central/Channel 4). He also presented the Channel 4 documentary about the death of Quentin Crisp. Tim is also the author of two books, *Quentin Crisp: a Biography* (Absolute Press) and the upcoming *Rude Britannia* (Weidenfeld and Nicolson).

For up-to-date information, visit: www.timfountain.co.uk

Other titles in this series

SO YOU WANT TO BE A PLAYWRIGHT?

How to Write a Play and Get It Produced

Tim Fountain

NICK HERN BOOKS
London
www.nickhernbooks.co.uk

A Nick Hern Book

SO YOU WANT TO BE A PLAYWRIGHT?
first published in Great Britain in 2007
by Nick Hern Books Limited
14 Larden Road, London w3 7st

Cover designed by Peter Bennett

Typeset by Country Setting, Kingsdown, Kent, ct14 8es
Printed and bound in Great Britain by Biddles, King's Lynn

A CIP catalogue record for this book
is available from the British Library

ISBN 978 1 85459 716 8

For Alan Greenhalgh

*without whom I would never
have 'got to the end'*

Acknowledgements

I'd like to thank all the people I've worked with over the years and whose ideas I have no doubt 'borrowed' for this book. And thanks to Richard Allen.

Tim Fountain

Contents

INTRODUCTION

The Story Only You Know

What is the difference between a writer with a play on stage and a writer who never sees their work produced? Is it talent? Well, perhaps; although I'm sure you have seen plays in which the writer displays no discernible talent whatsoever. Is it luck? Maybe; though I still prefer to believe the theory that you make your own luck. No, the biggest difference between the writer who is produced and goes on to be successful, and the one who isn't, is that they actually *got to the end*. However many hours you devote to the understanding of dramatic structure, however many seminars you attend by story gurus, however accomplished as a playwright you become and however many plays of your own you actually get to see on the stage, the hardest part of writing is actually *getting to the end*.

Throughout most of my career I have only finished plays because I have been frightened by deadlines: seeing the posters being displayed or the production dates listed in theatre brochures, being pressurised by directors, or investing my own money and needing it back. I've always had huge difficulty in writing plays in the abstract sense, without a support network or a clear destination for the end product in my mind. It's no coincidence that many of our most successful and prolific playwrights ran or run their own companies, or have produced and invested in their own work (Shakespeare, Noël Coward, Alan Ayckbourn, John Godber to name just a few).

As someone once said, there is nothing like the fear of imminent execution for concentrating the mind. Left to their own devices, most writers will prevaricate as long as possible and, when they do actually start writing, will delay the point where they show the play to others – the 'Day of Judgement', if you like – as long as possible. How many times have you spent months rewriting the first twenty pages of your work, despite knowing in your heart of hearts that until you reach the end you will never know whether those first twenty pages matter or are merely the backstory to the main event? How many plays have you begun and then abandoned halfway through? How many times has a good idea drowned in the sea of your self-doubt? And how many times has jealousy eaten you up when you have seen others succeed with a story that you wanted to tell two years before but didn't quite manage to? Well, now say to yourself out loud these words: 'Never again.'

I am going to get you to write that play and no excuses will be accepted. You work full time, you have children to bring up. Tough. If you want it enough, you will find the time and space, and this book will help you. It will take you from the genesis of your idea through to the final production of your play. From deciding whether your idea is worth pursuing to spotting which producer to send your script to, or which director might be the right one to direct your work. I will try and give you ideas, spur you on, ask you the right questions at relevant points, but above all else I will try to *get you to the end* and to *tell the story only you know.*

*

The story only you know is the story that *you* and *only you* could write in this way. It is a story with an emotional land-scape that is yours and only yours. It is the story that will not go away and burns inside you. It is a story that you have to tell – not because you think it would make a good part for a particular actor, or sell well in the West End (though that's an obvious bonus) – but because you have to get the damned thing out. It is the story about which you can offer *insight,* not just *opinion.*

There is a crucial difference between the two. Most of us have an opinion on many things; let's say America, its people and its politics, but without spending time in the country we cannot offer insight. No newspaper worth its salt would dream of having a foreign correspondent living outside the country they are meant to be reporting from. Of course that doesn't mean that in order to write about a murderer you need to take to the streets and hack someone to pieces, but it does mean that you have to believe you can understand this person, get inside their heads and, crucially, not simply judge them from the outset. Words like 'bad', 'mad', 'evil' or 'wicked' are of little use to the playwright, since they imply a one-dimensional view of life. It is your job to find the good in the evil and of course the evil in the good.

So before embarking on the long, difficult and often tortuous journey of writing a play ask yourself the fundamental question: 'Do I really know about this subject, these people, this world?' That doesn't mean you have to have met your characters in the flesh or write autobiographically (though the old adage that we write best about that which we know still holds true), but it does mean that plays cannot be written at arm's length. You will have to roll up your sleeves and get stuck in, because your unique way of seeing the world is what the audience craves. However strong your craftsmanship, however deep your understanding of dramatic structure or careful your research or profound your intellect, all of it will count for nothing if your work is inauthentic. An audience wants to hear *your voice*, they want to see your vision of the world, and they want *the story only you know*.

This demand often frightens people. Inside their heads a little voice cries out: 'How can my view of the world, how can my ideas, how can my feelings be of interest to others?' Well, if you are honest, if you tell it like *you* see it (not as you think the audience wants to see it), then you will be of interest to others. But if you fake it, if you lie to yourself, if you mire yourself in endless plot twists and obfuscation, their attention will soon drift away. Another voice that often pops into the writer's mind at the outset of writing is the one that screams: 'I will never be as good a writer as Ibsen or Miller! How can my plays stand up alongside those by Churchill or Stoppard?' To this I would say two things. Firstly, don't forget they were once starting out just like you, and they too had to make the leap of faith in themselves that I am asking you to make; and secondly, for every person who thinks Harold Pinter is a theatrical genius, there will be another who can't bear his 'obscure' work and is waiting to see a play by someone just like you. Great writers didn't beam down from another planet. They are living, breathing people from our world, who had the willpower and the talent to tell their stories.

PART ONE

Getting Started

Storytelling

The good storyteller

Think about the people you know. Think about the characters in your life that command the most attention, the ones who garner the most laughs when they tell a story. Are they the cleverest people you know? The most highly educated? The most articulate? Perhaps, but more likely they are the ones who are simply the best storytellers, whose stories you believe because they have the hot stink of authenticity.

But why do they have this authenticity? I believe it's because the person doing the telling dares to be himself or herself. This seldom involves self-glorification (except by default because they have entertained others); often the stories told by good storytellers will be *against* themselves. The time they ended up drunk with X, bought a car with no engine from Y, fell in love foolishly with Z. No one wants to hear tales of extraordinary success – unless it was achieved against all odds and with a considerable price paid along the way. Far more appealing to an audience is when the storyteller has the confidence to reveal his or her failings. In doing so, they square with us, they become one of us, they tell us that our vulnerability is shared by them, they speak universally, they confirm we are part of a society, and they make us feel less isolated as human beings.

Releasing the story only you know

Many writers start out writing highly autobiographical plays. So perhaps you should begin by looking at what is closest to you. Look at the stories in your everyday life. Think about the myths handed down through your family. The stories you remember most clearly from your school days. Could you take the kernel of them and expand it into a play? Perhaps there is a full story there already? Are there missing pieces to the tales that you could fill in to create a play? Is there a character from your past who fascinates you, whose voice you can hear clearly and around whom you could construct a story? Do you have regrets about things you did or didn't do that you wish to examine? Do you sometimes fantasise about leaving your lover? Taking a lover? Giving up your job? How your life would be now had you made a different decision at a crucial crossroads? All of these things may inspire a play.

However, this approach may be too directly autobiographical for some: you may find yourself unable to free yourself from the 'vérité' of your actual life. After all, you must never let the facts get in the way of a good story. If this is the case then you may find the following exercise useful. It is an exercise designed to release a very personal story in a very simple way. But before we look at it we need to define some terms so that when we use them later on they mean the same thing to each of us.

Definitions

CHARACTER   *Decision under pressure.* Characters are not what they say they are, but what they *do*, and what they do is prompted by the decisions the narrative and the other characters force them to make. For example, Iago in *Othello* says he's honest; what he does is the exact opposite. Character only emerges through action, and action is decision under pressure.

INNER CONFLICT   *Conflict between the person and themselves.* For example, Lear wants to accept what Cordelia says at the beginning of *King Lear* but is too insecure to do so. Willy Loman in Arthur Miller's *Death of a Salesman* wants to stop selling but doesn't believe he has achieved enough.

INTER-PERSONAL CONFLICT   *Conflict between people and others.* For example, Romeo and Juliet and their parents; Lear and his daughters; Willy Loman and his sons; Shirley Valentine and her (offstage) husband in Willy Russell's play.

EXTRA-PERSONAL CONFLICT *Conflict between people and their world.* For example, a woman in a patriarchal society; a Muslim in an Islamophobic country; Willy Loman and the American Dream.

INCITING INCIDENT *The moment without which the story would not exist. It is often something that destabilises the protagonist and compels them to go into action. It should be at least in part generated by the inner conflict of the protagonist.* For example, Lear banishes Cordelia because she refuses to tell him what he wants to hear, but also because his character will not allow him to accept her public behaviour. Shirley Valentine accepts the invitation from her friend to go on holiday to Greece, but deep down has doubts about whether it's the right thing to do, which affects her behaviour.

SCENE *A unit of action in which something changes.*

ACT CLIMAX *A major change, shift or reversal, the sum total of the scenes that precede it* (nothing to do with intervals or curtains coming down!). For example, C.S. Lewis in William Nicholson's *Shadowlands* acknowledges that he is in love with someone, having always denied he needs love.

CRISIS *A moment of decision forced upon the protagonist by the narrative.* It should not be an easy choice and whichever decision they make should have disadvantages as well as advantages. For example, Nora leaving Torvald in Ibsen's *A Doll's House.* She may have found her voice, escaped her unhappy domestic circumstances, but she has also given up her safe life for an unknown one as a single woman in a society not tolerant of such behaviour. It is by no means an easy choice, nor risk-free.

CLIMAX *What happens as a result of the decision taken in the crisis, and a logical outcome of the train of events set in motion by the inciting incident.* For example, Lear banished Cordelia; result: he effectively kills her. Shirley Valentine went on holiday without her husband; result: she is forced to decide between staying in Greece and risk losing him, or going back home and forfeiting all she has gained.

RESOLUTION *When the deeper meaning of the story becomes apparent.* Even though, as Samuel Goldwyn famously said, 'Pictures are for entertainment, messages should be delivered by Western Union', the resolution is where the writer's underlying meaning is most clearly heard. The resolution is the last moment that the audience experience and a strong part of what they take away with them from the story. For example, in *Shadowlands*, C.S. Lewis preaches a sermon to his congregation in which he flatly contradicts what he said to them at the beginning of the story, accepting that even though the only woman he has ever loved has died, it is better to have loved and lost than never to have loved at all. Shirley Valentine's husband decides to come to Greece and see his wife on *her* terms.

Definitions out the way, let's return to our exercise:

Character and inner conflict

1 Try and recall a situation in your life – it could be in the distant past or within the last hour – when you did or said something you didn't mean to. Not because of a slip of the tongue or ignorance or because anyone else compelled you to, but because of your character (you!) *acting under pressure.* You may have wanted to ask a girl or guy out but didn't. You may have wanted to apologise to someone but didn't. You may have bullied someone when really you meant to be tender.

2 Now ask yourself a deeper question. What was really going on there? Why did I do what I did? The answer to this question cannot be 'Because they made me do it' or 'Because my father kicked the cat when I was twelve' (though he may well have done and we will return to this later). I want you to find the answer that is ultimately your nature, or your nature which, at that time, was acting under pressure.

3 I want you to boil the incident down to two very specific things: your *goal* (what you wanted to do) and the *obstacle* (what stopped you from doing it that was nobody's fault except your own). For example, the goal:

asking the girl out; the obstacle: your fear of rejection. Of course there are many other reasons you could come up with for why you failed to achieve your goal: 'I didn't feel worthy of her', 'I was too proud to do the asking', 'I was worried about the financial cost', 'I didn't know where to take her' . . . But what you *must* do is come up with the *single* answer that was absolutely true of you at that moment.

Often when I've worked through this exercise in a classroom situation, students feel very exposed and blush when I press them for the real reason they failed to achieve their goal. When we do arrive at the answer, they feel ashamed, as if I have revealed them to be some sort of emotional inadequate. Often they will say, 'But I'm not normally like that' or 'It never happened again' (even if that's not the case and, on closer examination, they repeat this behaviour in many different areas of their lives).

But what is always most fascinating is when I ask the rest of the class if they have ever done the same thing, and made the same 'error' under pressure. Invariably, every hand in the room goes up. Who amongst us has not experienced failing to ask someone out because of the fear of rejection? Answer: no one. Some of us may have spent a lifetime doing it – like a character from one of Alan Bennett's *Talking Heads* – or some of us may have only done it once with massive consequences. But by being specific, by revealing a truth about him or herself, the playwright will have tapped into a universal truth. They felt they were revealing some terrible secret about their inner psyche when in fact they were holding a mirror up to the rest of the group, their audience. They dared to be themselves. Thus, they have sown the seeds of a story and, more importantly, created a character with universal appeal. Yet we know nothing of this character aside from his goal and the obstacle which prevented them from following it through. How can this be? The answer lies in character and the nature of character in drama.

*

Firstly, it's important to grasp that character in drama is very different from character in life. Put on stage a person with a thousand contradictions (as we often perceive ourselves to have), with all those contradictions playing out at once, and you will almost certainly have a mess of a play with no character and no drama. But put on stage a person who makes specific decisions as a result of *inner conflict* acting upon him or her, and character will emerge.

Character is *decision under pressure*, and it cannot emerge without both pressure and decision (even if the decision is to avoid decision, as in the case of Hamlet). In drama, as in life, we are not what we say we are, we are what we *do*. I may tell you I am a selfless person, but if under pressure I choose to put myself first, then that is what you will rightly deduce to be my character – unless I later prove otherwise, and even then doubts will linger in your mind about me. However, if a character simply makes the decisions he or she wants to make, or has to make, under the pressure of the narrative then you are in danger of creating a fairy story, and a character like James Bond or Cinderella. In these examples, the central character has few dimensions and exists simply to achieve the goals they want to achieve (save the planet or marry the prince).

When your characters have inner conflict (in our earlier example, the fear of rejection when asking someone out) then they become three-dimensional, interesting creations, and an audience will be compelled to watch them. The central narrative of Richard Curtis's romantic comedy film *Notting Hill*, for instance, is generated from just such a simple central inner conflict. Hugh Grant's character is incapable of asking out Julia Roberts because he doesn't think he is up to it, and from this conflict springs his (albeit slim) character and the whole plot – and indeed other Richard Curtis/Hugh Grant movies based on similar conflict, like *Four Weddings and a Funeral* and *Love Actually*.

Shadowlands, William Nicholson's TV play (later a stage play and then a film starring Anthony Hopkins) about the writer C.S. Lewis is generated from a very clear central inner contradiction on the part of its protagonist at the start of the story. Lewis has never fallen in love and lives with his brother in the groves of academia. Along comes a woman who wants to love him, and he struggles hard to resist, oppressed by his innate conservatism and fear of change. But he succumbs, takes the risk, falls in love, and develops as a person, before tragically discovering his lover is dying. Having never loved before, he is now forced to deal with love and grief, another conflict. The central question the play poses – Is it better to have loved and lost than never to have loved at all? – is resolved at the conclusion. Lewis, who preached otherwise at its outset, tells his congregation that grief is the price we pay for love and that it is a price worth paying.

In the first scene of *King Lear*, the ageing monarch divides his kingdom between his three daughters, Goneril, Regan and Cordelia. He asks each to profess their love for him in front of the court. Goneril and Regan fawn and flatter. Cordelia is more forthright and says that she loves him 'according to [her] bond; no more nor less'. Now if he'd had fewer 'issues', Lear could have said, 'Thank you, Cordelia, here's your third.' Then there'd be no difficulty, no play. But he doesn't. He can't. His inner conflict, his vanity, his neediness – call it what you will – makes him demand more from her and when she refuses to give it, he banishes her, thus removing from his life the daughter who loves him most and putting himself at the mercy of those who have least time for him. The whole narrative arc is launched from a seemingly small incident at the start of the play which is, in turn, generated from Lear's inner conflict.

Many years ago I recall seeing a play by Richard Cameron set in the mining community of South Yorkshire, and over-hearing two Sloaney teenage girls discussing it in the interval. One said to the other, 'Oh my gosh! The father in the play is just like Daddy.' I thought to myself, 'But he is nothing like your daddy. He is working class, he is from a different part of the country, he speaks in a vernacular that could not be further removed from yours ... ' And then I worked out what she meant. The scene we had witnessed on stage was one in which the father tried desperately, but unsuccessfully, to tell his son what he felt about him. The inner conflict – the desire to express feeling and the inability to do so – had created a universal character capable of speaking to miners from South Yorkshire and minors from South Kensington.

*

It's fine to begin writing from a position of indignation about the political system you or someone else lives in (extra-personal conflict). It's human to be angry at those who mistreat others either deliberately or inadvertently (inter-personal conflict). But in all my experience as a literary manager and reader of scripts, the primary level, the inner conflict, is the one too often missing.

Those other levels of conflict are necessary and can make for good drama, but unless your characters are also victims of themselves and their own nature, they will prove unconvincing, with no backstory, and nothing for the actors to sink their teeth into. When actors talk about great parts, I believe that this is what they are looking for: inner demons, personal contradictions and behavioural flaws that propel their character inexorably towards the play's conclusion. Both King Lear and Willy Loman suffer from a surfeit of pride and this prevents them from admitting their errors and seeking help until it is too late. The cause of this pride may be different for each character, but the net result is much the same. The inability to seek help fuels the narrative and keeps the ball in the air dramatically, as they journey further and further from the course which the audience wishes they would take.

No actor worth their salt wants simply to play a victim of others; it's the theatrical equivalent of becoming a whipping post. Much better to combine the role of victim with that of someone deluding themselves, for example. Then something might just catch fire.

Inner conflict is a phrase I shall return to, time and time again throughout this book. I believe it's what creates great characters and, hence, parts great actors want to play, and also I believe it is what will generate the narrative for you and help you get to the end.

All the time I hear writers saying that creating the story is the hardest part for them. Forget the story, cut the 'outside-in' thinking while you try to invent a plot, and do some thinking from the 'inside-out'. Look at the characters deeply, make them their own worst enemies. Ask yourself what they'd do next in any given situation, force them to make decisions under pressure, take risks and then the story will occur organically.

Think about a time when you had a clear objective – to apologise, to reprimand, to woo, to seduce, to say no, to say yes – and you didn't do it. And then ask yourself 'why?' Now you must be tough with yourself. You can't be a playwright without examining what your friends call 'the trouble with you'. The answer cannot be solely because someone else wouldn't let you or society wouldn't allow it, but because of something inside you and you must boil it down to something an actor could play in an improvisation. For example, I could tell an actor to woo a girl in the rehearsal room, but if I then said, 'The problem you have is that you weren't loved enough by your mother, your father left at an early age, you were bullied at school and your social class is a worry to you,' the whole thing will be almost impossible to play, it will become mired in complication. However, if I say you are bullish or proud or shy or vain, and combine this with the same objective, then an actor can play the scene and both character and action will emerge. From this action a backstory will offer itself to both performer and their audience. Why is he so bullish? Is he masking his fear? Why is he proud? Is that just a ruse? What makes him shy? Was he let down in the past?

I cannot emphasise enough that these character traits and this implied past will only emerge if the character has a clear objective in a scene and pursues it with his or her inner conflict acting upon them. This inner conflict will generate both the present-tense narrative and the backstory. Importantly, it will be a backstory serving that narrative, not imposed on the story like a checklist or a fake CV created in a sterile environment.

Character is perpetual action, and action can only occur when a character has a goal and something preventing him or her from achieving it. David Mamet famously said, 'People may or may not say what they mean . . . but they *always* say something designed to get what they want.' An oversimplification perhaps, but a rule better followed too closely than rejected out of hand. Plays may be carried largely by dialogue but that dialogue must never be chatter; it has to relate to the pursuit of a goal, be it conscious or unconscious (or both). Try and train your ear, when you listen to the conversations of others, to work out what they are *really* saying. Is the man at the bus stop who always mentions the weather simply a bore or is he trying to make a connection? Is the girl who says she never wants to marry protesting too loudly? Why does the father always reprimand his son publicly? Characters – and plays – are like icebergs; only a small amount shows above the surface. You have to become an expert at knowing the whole shape of your creation, and knowing what to reveal and what to withhold.

*

So let's return to our example. The boy wanted to ask the girl out, but didn't do it because he feared rejection. Here you have the beginnings of a scene, and with the beginnings of a scene you have the beginnings of an act, and with it a whole story. Now in order for the exercise to work it's important to be strong, simple and accurate. Don't have twenty reasons why he didn't ask the girl out. Pin it down to one.

Try improvising the scenario. The person playing the boy knows his goal is to ask the girl out; he knows his obstacle is the fear which prevents him from doing it. The essential ingredients of a scene are all there, character should start to emerge and, with it, a narrative. The dialogue can be as simple as this:

HE: Hi.

SHE: Hi.

HE: I like your jeans.

SHE: Thanks.

HE: Where d'you get them?

SHE: Topshop.

HE: Right. I like Topshop. It's cheap, isn't it?

SHE: Very.

HE: But quite cool.

SHE: Very.

   Beat.

   Well, I better be going.

HE: Oh.

SHE: I've got a lecture at eleven.

HE: Oh right. What?

SHE: Boring sociology.

HE: Shit.

SHE: Exactly. Well, I'll see you around then.

HE: Yes. (*Beat.*) Bye.

SHE: Bye.

It's not the most scintillating dialogue ever written, but it contains all the essential ingredients of dramatic writing:

NARRATIVE	A boy attempts to ask a girl out.
INTENTION	He has a clear objective in the scene to ask the girl out, even though it is never stated.
OUTCOME	He fails in his objective and leaves the scene without saying what he wants to say.
SUBTEXT	He talks about Topshop instead of what he wants to talk about – but we sense what he (and perhaps she) really wants.
CHARACTER	He is shy and not sexually confident.

It is clear at the beginning of the scene what the boy wants. He pursues the girl but is unable to express what he really wants to say; thus, his character emerges – and so does hers – and by the end of this briefest of scenes we have an outcome – he fails to ask her out – which will propel us into the next scene. All this was created knowing nothing of who these people are or where they are from, but from simply knowing what he wanted and the inner conflict which was preventing him getting it. Try writing your own version with the same objectives and outcomes.

*

We can now ask ourselves what someone who fears rejection does after this brief scene. Do they go and get drunk and make themselves unattractive to the object of their desires, thus pushing them further away? Do they turn to someone unsuitable but who makes all the running, thereby allowing them to get a partner without risking rejection? Do they feel even more insecure about their attractiveness and seek solace in casual sex with someone who places them in danger? There is of course no right answer as to what happens next. The joy of writing is that you – 'playing God' and listening to your own inner voice – can make the next decision for the character. However, there are 'wrong' decisions and these are worth examining.

A wrong decision would be the boy succeeding in asking the girl out in Scene 2. Why is this wrong? Firstly, because you have changed your character for no reason. They are suddenly able to do what they seemed unable to do in the previous scene although nothing in the narrative has occurred to change them. Secondly, you have shot yourself in the foot in narrative terms. Solving your character's 'inner conflict' (his desire for the girl versus his fear of rejection) within two scenes has killed off the potential for the development of your story. What you want to do is send your character on a journey away from themselves and what they truly need and desire.

This journey is what generates the audience's empathy for the character. They will see his true nature in Scene 1, so even if he's shagging a score of Nubian prostitutes in Scene 8, they still care because they have seen and know that, deep down, this is not his true character. Knowing the character from the outset also creates an expectation for the audience. They feel they know the type of person your character is, and what he wants after Scene 1; his universality being derived from the fact that all of us at some stage in our lives will have failed to ask someone out because we feared rejection. And yet he now seems to be going further and further away from his true needs as a result of this small failure. The audience might think it'll end in tears (tragedy), or that he will go on making the same mistakes for ever with increasingly ludicrous consequences (comedy), or that he will discover the truth about himself (classical drama), or face up to his demons and heroically overcome them (Hollywood). In short, each audience member starts to project into the future, involving themselves in the ensuing narrative. Will the expectations for the boy be met? What will happen to the girl? The audience starts to *care*. From the slightest source (the failure to ask someone out), we have started to generate a story which, whether it ends in tragedy or redemption, has *potential*.

*

Deny your characters self-knowledge until the narrative teaches it to them. Make them their own worst enemy in dramatic terms. Remember that in life it takes us a long time to learn that what we really needed and should have done was to marry or divorce, leave our small town or return to it. No matter how obvious it may be to those around us, we are all innately conservative creatures and stick to what we know, like drinkers to their bottle, even when it is clear we may be destroying our lives. This is a great help to the playwright. For Shakespeare, it means he can send Lear to the point of oblivion, strip him naked on the heath, and subject him to the most elemental forces of nature before he learns his lesson. Because it's tragedy, Lear's inner conflict, his tragic flaw – the inability to see that Cordelia loves him – causes him to destroy the thing he most loves and needs in the world. 'Why should a dog, a horse, a rat have life, and thou no breath at all?' Lear incredulously asks over his daughter's dead body. The answer is because he himself engineered it by his inability to accept her expression of love for him at the start of the play.

The key to the ending of any story is often in that inciting incident at the start, a 'wrong' turning taken by the central character or characters. Although, of course, this wrong turning can ultimately prove to be the best thing they have ever done. In Willy Russell's *Shirley Valentine*, Shirley decides after much prevarication to go on holiday to Greece with her best mate and leave her brutish husband at home. She is initially punished: her friend runs off with a man the minute she gets there and Shirley is left to dine alone, feeling like a fish out of water. But eventually, bit by bit, she learns to appreciate this solitude and then discovers (after a fling with a fisherman on a boat) that she does not wish to return to England and to her old life. The story has gone from a negative situation at the beginning (trapped with brute at home) to a positive one (risks going on holiday with friend) to a negative one (left alone on holiday) to a positive one (has fling with fisherman) to a further positive (deciding to stay in Greece and wait for her husband to visit her on her terms). But it all stems from the one inciting incident near the start of the play.

Begin your story not with an earthquake but with a small decision and follow its consequences through logically. Keep your protagonist active. Keep them making decisions. Put them in emotional or literal territory with which they are unfamiliar. Let them make mistakes. Let them change for worse and for better, and let them come out of the story at the end with a different – though not necessarily clearer or better – understanding of their world. Then you will have created a powerful narrative with universal appeal.

What kind of play do you want to write?

Tragedy, comedy, romance, thriller, a whodunnit, a whydunnit . . . ? There are numerous types of plays, and I think it's a mistake to begin your journey by predetermining the genre you are going to write in. It limits the scope of your imagination and the range of your characters. You put yourself in a straitjacket, and ignore the fact that the greatest tragedies contain moments of high comedy; the best romances can also be tragic. When you tell the man on the bus that you are a playwright, he will invariably ask what sort of plays you write. I would suggest the answer you give is 'Good ones.' Let the critics and academics decide what kind of dramatist you are. Your job is to be true to yourself. Having said that, it is perhaps worth looking at the different types of plays currently being produced, to get a feel for what's out there.

The singular original voice

By far the most common play produced in the English-speaking world is that created by the 'singular original voice'. Whilst there have been honourable exceptions to this rule (for example, *Pravda* by both Howard Brenton and David Hare, or *Sleeping Around* by Hilary Fannin, Stephen Greenhorn, Abi Morgan and Mark Ravenhill), most successful plays tend to be written by a single writer and are original in their content. Some recent examples would be *Art* by Yasmina Reza, which uses the purchase of a work of modern art as a springboard to examine the relationships between three long-term friends; Martin McDonagh's *The Beauty Queen of Leenane*, which uses a melodramatic form to dissect a corrosive relationship between a mother and daughter; and Sarah Kane's *4:48 Psychosis*, which examines the author's own neurosis through a fragmented, poetic approach. All have been successes as a result of a very particular vision, well expressed. Whilst all are wildly different in form and content, they share the unmistakeable mark of the author's own voice.

The plays of John Osborne – which, it's often claimed, gave birth to the 'modern age of British Drama' – eloquently express truths about the age in which he lived, but always refracted through the shattered lens of Osborne's own psyche. Richard Bean has written several plays closely based on familiar environments and past experiences: his time working in a Hull bread factory (*Toast*), amongst Hull trawlermen (*Under the Whaleback*) or on a farming community (*Harvest*). All of these writers have undoubtedly written about worlds about which they know, either literally or metaphorically.

Think about unusual places you may have worked or visited. Enclosed spaces where disparate characters were brought together. Could a place or a situation inspire a story? Never underestimate an audience's appetite for seeing worlds on stage they have not seen before. There may not be any new stories, as the old adage goes, but there are certainly new worlds opening up all the time. You may be the person to put them on stage.

Political theatre

Maybe you see yourself as a 'political' playwright, and you long to write a 'state of the nation' play. You want to be like one of the two divine Davids – Hare or Edgar – fired up with indignation about a particular subject. Maybe you are driven to write by the injustice of Third World debt repayments or the failings of New Labour. Maybe you are determined to expose the corruption that lies at the heart of modern life. You will still be compelled to populate your drama with three-dimensional people who eat, sleep and shit in the same way as your audience. If you do not do that, you will merely create a drama consisting of mouthpieces, full of 'sound and fury signifying nothing'. David Hare said there were two types of playwright: on the one hand, the one who practised 'inside-out' thinking, and on the other, the one who practised 'outside-in' thinking. He very accurately said that the former tends towards self-indulgence, and the latter tends towards unreality. In plays like *Racing Demon* about the Church of England or *The Permanent Way* about the state of British railways, Hare successfully examines areas of contemporary life with journalistic accuracy and a strong sense of moral indignation, but manages to populate the plays with contradictory characters that fine actors want to play. He is also unafraid of giving characters with whom he does not sympathise some of the best lines.

I have read many plays in which a playwright quite rightly wished to elicit sympathy from his audience for a character who is victim of the system, such as a miner cast aside by Thatcherism or a soldier made to fight an unjust war. But they fail to create a protagonist with universal appeal because they merely make them a victim of larger external forces. You have to find what it is specifically that made that person subscribe to the system in the first place. Maybe the soldier wanted to be the perfect son and that's why he joined the army and went to war. Maybe he did it because his brother died in action and he wants to appear heroic. Maybe he never wanted to join the army but his father accused him of being a 'nancy boy' and so he wants to prove his masculinity. Maybe he wanted to wear a uniform in order to increase his self-esteem or to impress his girlfriend. Now, with motivation and inner conflict and characters, we have a play about the injustice of war that an audience, most of whom have never been near a war zone, can relate to.

Documentary theatre

The Tricycle Theatre in north London has been at the forefront of this movement and, in recent years, has enjoyed great success with fine productions of Richard Norton-Taylor's plays: *Nuremberg* (recreating the war-crimes trial); *The Colour of Justice* (taken from an inquiry into the police investigation of the murder of Stephen Lawrence, a young black Londoner); *Justifying War* (an abridgement of the Hutton Inquiry into the government's case for invading Iraq); and *Called to Account* (a fictional hearing debating whether or not former Prime Minister Tony Blair is indictable for war crimes against Iraq).

These plays are all based not only on extant material concerning the subject matter – be that court documents or government papers – but on interviews with real people which have subsequently been edited and put on the stage.

Verbatim theatre

Verbatim plays are a very close relative of documentary theatre. Here the author concentrates exclusively on interviewing people directly involved in real situations and then transforms the material into a play. Significant examples are *Talking to Terrorists* by Robin Soans, *The Permanent Way* by David Hare, and Alecky Blythe's *Come On Eli* and *Cruising*, both of which take it a step further by having the actors faithfully reproduce on stage, literally verbatim, the interviews as they listen to them on headsets.

It would be advisable to approach a theatre or management before you actually embark on a play like this. It is such a specific project and requires so much work that you wouldn't want to spend a year-and-a-half of your life on it only to find that no one wanted to produce it, by which stage the subject matter has ceased to be 'hot' or have any relevance to a contemporary audience.

Monologues

Monologue is a form that I have worked with a great deal and one that appeals to me greatly. A good monologue delivered by a skilled actor is an experience like no other in the theatre. As an audience, we are being addressed directly; artifice seemingly disappears. It is less a night at the theatre, in a traditional sense, and more like being 'at home' with the character. I have seen audiences watching monologues actually respond to the actor on stage as if they were a real person answering their questions, investing in their hopes. On the other hand, a bad monologue in the hands of a poor actor provides the most excruciating theatregoing experience of your life. We quickly decide in the theatre whether we like an actor and whether we like what he or she has to tell us. The agony of knowing after the first five minutes that we are not interested in this person and that no other person will emerge to relieve our agony can make ninety minutes seem like a hundred years in solitary.

Monologue is its own particular form. While there is considerable overlap with the techniques of traditional playwriting (beginning, middle, end; speeches which sound authentic, etc.), there are specific things that anyone setting out to write a successful monologue should think about. Principal amongst these is the question: 'Is my narrator a reliable witness?' Far too many monologues are crippled with an honest protagonist whose view of the story they are in and the world around them is alarmingly accurate and coincides with that of the playwright. This results in a one-dimensional play with no depth and none of the dynamism that arises from dramatic irony where the audience know more than the character on stage. Alan Bennett in his wonderful *Talking Heads* series (originally written for television but subsequently staged) is a master of the unreliable witness. Graham in *A Chip in the Sugar* is an unmarried middle-aged man living with his mother, telling his audience the story of her failed affair with a charlatan. We are constantly aware that she was duped, that the central character suspected so all along – but also he willed it to be so, and that the story he tells us is very much his version of events told from the perspective of someone who does not wish his mother to have a relationship. He is both right and wrong all at the same time. This gives the monologue an element of conflict – precisely what so many monologues lack, given the absence of other characters present to give their sides of the story. The conflict in this case being the gulf between the truth and Graham's version of it, which makes the audience active participants. We are not merely passive spectators to the story but are called upon to interpret it, to make judgements about the person who is telling it, and to decide for ourselves what really happened.

In the monologues I wrote about Quentin Crisp (*Resident Alien*) and Julie Burchill (*Julie Burchill is Away* . . .) the audience were called upon to decide whether these characters were as happy and fulfilled as they claimed they were. I avoided the moment where they broke down in tears and told the audience their lives were a sham, that fame was an empty vessel and that all they wished they'd really done was open a knitting shop in Carlisle. The conflict came between what they said to the audience, and their physicality and actions which told a contrasting story. For example, Crisp lectured on style whilst frying an egg in his squalid flat; Burchill told us how lucky she was whilst glugging large glasses of vodka.

One of the major failings of the one-person show based on a real-life person (which has become a stock-in-trade of the Edinburgh Fringe Festival) is the tedious trawl through the facts of the subject's life. You need to do the research, know those facts, but then discard them and leap to the emotional core of the character's life.

What I love most about monologues is that there is nowhere to hide and no way to lie – for either the actor or the playwright. The experience for the audience is akin to meeting someone in a bar and deciding whether or not what they have to say is credible and authentic, and if they are interesting. Monologues allow an actor to weave a magic spell on a group of people in the simplest possible way. It is elemental in its form, with its roots stretching back to an age when a strolling storyteller would roll up in the town and tell stories to captivate the crowd.

On a practical level, monologues have the huge advantage of being portable, instantly stageable in all kinds of eclectic venues, and needing little more than some lights and some seats. It is for that reason that many actors, frustrated by the powerlessness of long periods waiting for the phone to ring, write their own tailor-made show which they can tour themselves, making money between other jobs.

Historical plays

If you are writing an historical drama or a play about people who actually existed then research is obviously crucial. It is important to immerse yourself in as many different opinions about the subject and the people involved as possible. But there has to come a time when the research is thrown out the window, otherwise you will simply end up dramatising the research. As Alan Bennett said, 'Don't let the facts get in the way of the truth.'

I struggled with masses of historical information for my play *Tchaikovsky in the Park*, unable to find the story I wanted to tell, until one day I came across a diary entry that Tchaikovsky had written about fifteen years after the death of a boy. It was the longest diary entry Tchaikovsky had ever written about another person, and it was an outpouring of grief about the boy's suicide. There was a rumour that Tchaikovsky was having an affair with the boy at the time that he composed *Romeo and Juliet*, so I put the two things together and invented the rest. Tchaikovsky placed his desire to create music and enjoy social respectability above his desire for the boy. The boy ultimately paid the price; Tchaikovsky lived with the guilt. So whilst the play was based on fact, and an honest attempt to sum up the essence of the man, it was also largely invented.

If you are attempting to bring a 'real' character to life, the question you should ask yourself is 'If this were not Mary Queen of Scots but Mary Smith, not John F Kennedy but Jack Brown, would it be of interest to the audience?' In other words, does the character feature all the attributes previously discussed as being essential to good drama? Do they have objectives? Inner conflicts? Can you hear their voice? And does the drama you have created speak about the human condition or just the condition of the historical figures on stage? The fact that your characters actually existed once is no guarantee that they will come alive on stage. You will have to give us your version of them; in other words, 'invent' them just as you would a fictional character. Remember that your play is a work of fiction even if it is based on fact.

Alternative theatre

Maybe you are the kind of writer for whom the very word 'play' turns you off. Maybe you see yourself as a 'creator' of theatre. Maybe the interior-room set, French windows or pub door are anathema to you. Maybe when you conjure up a vision of your dream show, you see puppets, video screens, dancing, onstage musicians. Well, the same rules apply. Form is a means to express content and should not become an end in itself. Even in shows where the form is inseparable from the content, if you simply dazzle your audience with stage tricks, bright lights, inventive choreography and clever video-editing without telling them anything about what it is to be human, you will leave them unsatisfied. Whether you are a playwright or 'creator' of theatre, you will still have to hold a mirror up to society in your work. In order to do that, you will have to honestly examine your own relationship both with the story you are telling and with the world around you. Do not mistake saying something loudly and brightly for actually having something to say.

Inspirations

Where do you get your ideas from?

Somebody once remarked that 'Nothing beats life itself' – and it is true. No matter how fantastic the stories you create, no matter how vivid your imagination, you will never trump life itself. So keep your eyes and ears open, listen to your colleagues, your friends and your family. Scour newspapers and magazines. The successful playwright is always hungry for a new idea and is ready to draw inspiration from anywhere. Look inward to try and see your own life as others see it. See what may be dramatic about what you already know, territory about which you can provide insight not just opinion. Imagine yourself leading a different life, imagine having taken a different journey, turned different ways at crossroads. Always remember that you are writing *the story only you know.*

Many was the time when I was Literary Manager of The Bush Theatre in West London that I sat down with a writer over a drink and talked to them about their less-than-successful play, only to hear them tell a fantastic story about their friends, family or workplace and leaving me longing to see *that* play rather than the one they had written. And, of course, literary managers and directors have said the same to me as a writer. It's all about releasing the story you really want and need to tell. Often it is the material we are most familiar with that we wrongly assume is of little interest to others, that captures the imagination.

*

Most of the best playwrights have at some time 'stolen' material from other people. Harold Pinter was heavily influenced by black-and-white movies of the 1930s; in turn, Pinter's influence on Jez Butterworth, author of *Mojo*, has often been remarked on. Some of Alan Bennett's comic rhythms owe much to the music-hall routines that would have been watched by his parents. Martin McDonagh's plays are often described as a cross between Quentin Tarantino and J.M. Synge. John Godber's *Up 'n' Under* was a direct homage to the *Rocky* movies. Sometimes this 'stealing' is conscious, sometimes subconscious.

At other times, writers will steal ideas from their family history and from their friends. Don't be fearful of this. To begin with, you may try writing in the style of your heroes; it might be the only way for you to get going. Philip Larkin's first collection of poetry, *The North Ship*, was Yeatsian in form. He soon found his own, much more successful voice, but Yeats got him going.

How do you know if your idea is any good?

You don't.

And if I could give you a simple answer, I wouldn't. I would keep it to myself, go away and make my fortune. However, there's one crucial question to ask yourself before embarking on your writing journey, and it's one that may take you eighteen months or more to answer: 'Does this idea really excite me?' Not just intellectually but emotionally. Can you feel it in your gut? Is the feeling strong enough to sustain you through the hundreds of hours to come? If this were the last play you were allowed to write, is this what you would write? If there were only one hundred sheets of paper left in the world, is this what you would choose to fill them with?

If the answers to all these questions is a resounding and passionate 'Yes!', then I suggest you proceed regardless of what I am about to ask you or anyone else might tell you.

However, these other questions may be worth at least considering in your mind . . .

Considerations

Who is your play for?

If you feel in your heart of hearts that you *must* tell this story, then your play is 'for' you. But in order to avoid the dangers of self-indulgence I prefer to take the advice of Richard Cameron, who says he writes for 'the *me* in the audience'. That is to say that he writes the play he wants to write, but tries to imagine himself in a room full of other people watching it.

It is also worth giving some consideration as to whether there is an audience who wants to see the play you are about to devote such a lot of time and effort to. This is not about carrying out some exercise in market research, or falling into the trap of giving the audience what you *think* they want. It is about considering whether the story you intend to tell (and the way you want to tell it) intersects meaningfully with the society in which you and your audience exist and the times in which you all live. Writing a play may be a private act, but its ultimate worth will be established in a public arena. No good playwright exists in a vacuum.

Never forget that Shakespeare – by common consent the greatest of them all – wrote plays for specific theatres, specific actors and specific audiences. Given that he had to write to live, he knew the importance of his work chiming with his society. This is not about analysing the commercial aspects of your work but about facing up to your responsibility as an artist.

Does your play have something new to say?

This is a question that troubles many playwrights. The fear of being unoriginal seems to give younger dramatists, in particular, sleepless nights. It is often this fear that drives them headfirst into the arms of that least original of all types of work: the wilfully obscure. Fearful of being laughed at or 'found out', the artist creates a smokescreen of obscurity. Do not mistake creating work that is rich with the possibilities of different interpretation with the type of work that is fearful of nailing its colours to the mast lest it be accused of unoriginality. The best way of being universal is through the specific. Stick your neck out. Tell it like it is. Be accurate. If you are true to yourself and your vision of the world, if you believe utterly in the originality of your voice, then you will inevitably be saying something new to your audience.

That said, if your idea has been the subject matter of numerous recent plays there is a danger that, no matter how particular, your originality will not be noticed by audiences or critics, simply because they will feel they have seen it before. So it is vital that you maintain an awareness of what plays are being produced and the state of theatre more generally. You may not live in London, you may not be able to see all the new plays at the Royal Court, but most of us these days have access to the internet and you certainly have access to your local library. Through newspaper reviews, features and articles you can develop and maintain an understanding of where contemporary theatre is headed and of the work that is happening.

Never underestimate an audience's fascination with seeing worlds on stage that they have not seen before. When I was at The Bush Theatre we staged plays set in gay brothels, UN camps in the Third World, caravans on the West Coast of England. An audience loves the lights to come up on a location with which they are not familiar. And, similarly, the heart sinks if we get an immediate sense of déjà vu.

Should you know which theatre you are writing for?

Clearly if the play is commissioned by a specific theatre then only a fool would create something unsuitable for that space. If you are writing without any definite idea of which theatre your work could ultimately be staged in, then do not fret about the mechanics of how the play will function on stage. (Personally, I like to have some notion of where the play might fit, even if it is just that: a notion.) There will be plenty of time for directors and designers to get their heads round the problems you have created. In fact, in my experience many directors and designers actively *prefer* to work with playwrights who have created problems for them to solve. Designers, in particular, love the challenge of plays with multiple locations, in which scenes shift from interior to exterior sets.

Should you limit the size of your cast?

The smaller the cast, the more likely your play is to be produced. This is one of the major problems with the current theatre landscape: the proliferation of studio theatres (and the difficult economics of putting a new play in a big theatre) has encouraged a whole generation of writers to think small, both in terms of cast size and in terms of staging. As the Monsterist group of playwrights has quite rightly pointed out, if writers continue to create small plays for small places and small casts, then the whole notion of new plays on a grand scale will disappear from the theatrical lexicon. The group's manifesto is to elevate 'new theatre writing from the ghetto of the studio "black box" to the main stage'.

Nicholas Hytner, Artistic Director of the National Theatre, went on the record as saying he would like nothing more than to programme a play by a new writer in the 1100-seat Olivier Theatre (arguably the biggest and most significant stage in the UK) – and, indeed, David Eldridge's *Market Boy* was staged there in 2006. At London's Royal Court, Artistic Director Dominic Cooke has also called for plays that are Shakespearean in their scope, scale and ambition. So it could be that things are slowly changing . . .

If you are absolutely certain that your play requires a cast of fifteen plus, that you are not writing in a 'televisual' style, creating parts for actors which are tiny but designed to propel the plot forwards – then go ahead and think big.

Similarly, if you are writing for amateur companies, it may be a positive advantage to create more parts for all the people who want to get on the stage. But if your focus, as a first-time playwright, is 'getting it on' in the professional theatre, then it will be disingenuous of me not to recommend you try and limit the size of your cast to eight or fewer. Preferably fewer.

What if you can't write what you want?

You may not always be able to write exactly what you want. You may be called upon to write a play for a specific context or a specific group of people: entertainment for your local amateur theatre group, a sketch for the office party, a community play written for a specific group of people to perform in (and often about) a specific place. This does not mean that you should ignore your individual voice. When you are creating work that has specific boundaries it is even more important that you find 'yourself' in it.

In 1999 I was called on to write a play for the actor Bette Bourne to perform at the relatively small Bush Theatre. It was always envisaged the piece would be a one-man show utilising Bourne's unique talents as both a classically trained actor and a vaudevillian who really knows how to 'play' the audience and not hide behind the fourth wall. Beyond these parameters, I knew nothing. For a long time I flailed around, trying to find the right idea, until one day when I was having lunch with Bette and Mike Bradwell, the Artistic Director of The Bush at the time.

As we were tucking into our pudding (future producers note: Mr Bourne always has the pudding), the topic of our conversation turned to the great British eccentric Quentin Crisp. Bette did a little impression of him, having known him for twenty-five years. I had long been fascinated by Crisp and immediately seized on the idea of writing Bette's one-man show about him. Mike agreed that it was the right idea. Bette, however, wasn't convinced; he felt that John Hurt had already 'done' Quentin on film in *The Naked Civil Servant*, but both Mike and I felt very strongly that there was real mileage in getting Bette to do his Quentin and to tell the story of Quentin's New York years. Something excited us about the project. Bourne, like Crisp, had once had another name and persona but had jettisoned them in favour of one he felt more accurately characterised him. He had cast aside his old 'straight' clothes in favour of something much more flamboyant and outré. Like Quentin, Bette had created an artifice which became his essence. There was also something else which excited us hugely about the project: the idea of recreating Crisp's famously filthy and tiny New York apartment in the little jewel box that is The Bush Theatre.

At this time, not only had I never met Quentin Crisp but I also had never even been to New York. Very wisely, Mike Bradwell despatched me to the Big Apple to meet Quentin. Thereafter, despite the fact that the play was to be based on both his life and writing and therefore not entirely original in content, it became essential for me to find what it was in his story that meant something personally to me. Without this, the play would essentially have been a lifeless trawl through the facts of his life. In the end, after hundred of hours of reading his writing and meeting the man himself, I settled upon a very simple singular idea for a story which seemed to crystallise for me the essence of his life. I imagined a day when strangers that had arranged to meet him for lunch in order to discuss his thoughts on 'how to be happy' failed to show up. In so doing, I was able to test what I saw as the essential premise of Crisp's life: that what mattered was not what other people thought of you, but what you thought of yourself. When the production opened at The Bush, a friend who had seen a play of mine written ten years earlier pointed out that structurally the piece was identical to that. I realised that through *Resident Alien*, my play about Crisp, I inadvertently said what I had tried, less successfully, to say ten years earlier.

You might be called upon to create a play about the death of your local textile industry or your local call centre or to celebrate the centenary of your local brass band. Whilst it is important to do the research, to know something of the history, both factual and spiritual, of the subject about which you are writing, there should come a point where you cast aside that research and infuse the play with the spirit of you. Otherwise, it will be both an empty exercise and a soulless play. Your audience is not buying tickets to learn the date on which your local brass band was founded, the name of its founder or the colour of the rosette it won in the regional final in 1964. They are buying tickets to see, in the story of these particular characters in this particular situation, the truths of their own lives. Write honestly of the sorrows, fears and triumphs of these characters and the audience will be convinced that you have some unique window on their lives. A play is a lie that tells the truth; paradoxically, a play merely filled with 'truths' becomes an enormous lie.

Preparations

Should you plan your play before you start writing?

So you've got your idea. You feel passionate about it. You want to devote your time and energy to it, and you feel certain that it has something to say to you and to your audience. What should you do next? Should you map out the whole play with military precision, as some of the American screen-writing gurus would encourage you to do? Should you place giant colour-coded cards on your bedroom wall divided into categories: 'character', 'plot' and 'action'? Or should you simply write a line of dialogue and see where it takes you?

You must find the method that works best for you. And obviously if this is your first play you will have no idea what that is. So you will have to follow your gut instinct. If you decide you want to plan out your whole play before writing dialogue then do so. But if, when you start writing the play itself, you feel uninspired, the characters fail to take flight and the whole process begins to feel like hard work as opposed to play (and remember the word for the work you are writing is 'play'), then junk your plans and change your strategies. If you are the sort of writer who starts writing dialogue and after a few months ends up with lots of fragments but without the emergence of a play with the structure and muscularity needed to sustain a whole evening, then perhaps a bit of planning may be in order.

I think this is one of the most difficult of all areas and one of the most crucial decisions you will take during the whole process. Know too much about your play and where it is going and you may end up with a lifeless sprint. Know too little and you may end up with dialogue in search of a play. You will probably find that there is one of these two options or a combination of the two that will work best for you. My advice would be to go with the way of working that feels the most natural to you.

Having tried both methods, I favour just starting to write, though I like to have some idea of the shape of the 'skin' of my drama, some loose idea of where my characters are headed. I find that to know too much takes away my passion for the project and crucially my ability to write dialogue. So I tend to begin by just writing a scene, not necessarily the first scene, not necessarily a scene that will survive to the end of the final draft, but a scene I am passionate about, that I can feel in my gut, that is burning to come out. It may be the last scene of the play and that the subsequent work is back-tracking in order to find out how my characters got there and the events that lead up to this resolution. Or, if the scene is from the beginning of the play, what follows it? What would my characters do next? Many playwrights speak of that magical moment when the characters seem to take over the play and the writer feels like merely a conduit for their actions and thoughts. But above all else your objective at this stage is simply to *fill the pages!*

How much should you know about your characters?

Some writers prepare detailed character biographies; their approach is almost Stanislavskian. They want to know where the character comes from, what the character wears, and even, if they're particularly precise, what the character had for breakfast that morning. Other writers know nothing of their characters until they begin to speak. If I am writing an original play then I certainly favour the latter approach. For me, preparing a detailed character biography means I am then writing the play wearing a straitjacket, predetermining who my characters are and what they will do, and risking off-the-shelf characterisation and stock behaviour. I would far rather begin with a single line of dialogue that gets my juices flowing.

Recently I began a play with the line 'Fuck! I'm fucked.' Not perhaps the most poetic opening to a play and one that might have had Noël Coward spinning in his grave, but nonetheless a line which amused me, which captured the audience's attention, and, more importantly than all these things, brought a character onto the stage with a force field around him. Within those three simple words are implied a past (why is he fucked?), a present (he is fucked), and a future (what is he going to do about being fucked and how will others react?). For me, characterisation and writing dialogue is 'running with the ball', and the hardest bit is picking it up in the first place. I may struggle for ever to find three words as seemingly banal as 'Fuck! I'm fucked.' Once I have them, however, I have the catalyst to power my scene.

While writing my play about the columnist Julie Burchill, I struggled for ages to find her voice until one day I remembered something she had said to me on the phone: "'Ere, Tim, there is a man in Australia been killed by a jellyfish the size of a peanut!' In the play, I added to that line: 'Isn't that terrible? He was on his honeymoon as well. Really sad.' Suddenly I had captured the absurdity of her vision, her sense of humour, her intelligence and, perhaps more importantly, her impishness. And it would be this last quality, that teasing of those around her – and of the audience – that would fuel much of the one-person show. I know when I have been successful in creating characters: I can impersonate them in any context. I can make them speak about any subject. I can bring them to life in an instant.

The journey to this level of familiarity with your characters is a long one. Ibsen is reported as saying that in his first drafts his characters were like people he had met on a long train journey; with the second draft they were like people he'd spent a long weekend with in the country; and by the third draft they were like people he had known all his life. The difficult thing for a playwright is accepting the imperfection of those early drafts. The grating unfamiliarity that you feel towards your characters in the first draft can often drive you to despair and, more damagingly, lead to either repetitive rewrites or abandoning the project altogether. The world is full of half-finished plays. Don't add another to the pile.

Where do you find your characters' voices?

Well, they could be voices you have heard. They could be the voices of friends and family. I suspect that quite often they will be voices that recur over and over in your head, which you have little control over and little knowledge of how they got there. Do not be afraid of this. Many of the greatest writers' voices are instantly recognisable in play after play. One only has to hear a line of their dialogue to identify the work of Alan Bennett, Caryl Churchill or Harold Pinter. The fact that it is easy to mimic successful writers is far from an indictment: it is actually an affirmation of the clarity and distinctiveness of their voices. But it is also evidence that the number of characters they can inhabit is relatively limited.

Some writers take inspiration from photographs or photograph albums, newspaper pictures, paintings in art galleries, voices heard on buses or in markets. They may take their inspiration from a phrase they heard, maybe a line they remember from their childhood. Some can be inspired by an article of clothing, a pair of shoes or a hat. Some writers change posture in their chair according to which character they are writing. Does my character have a stiff back or does he slouch? Does she speak slowly or quickly? Does she think about what she's said or does she speak first and think later?

As in many aspects of playwriting, the key is simplicity. At least to begin with, give yourself a very clear, simple character onto which you can hang your voice. This is one reason why I think knowing too much about a character's biography is crippling. The phrase 'But my character wouldn't do that . . .' is completely meaningless at this stage. That is not to say, however, that your characters can do or say anything. If they demonstrate more self-knowledge or experience than the drama so far has accorded them, then you're effectively changing the character, and an audience won't go with it. By and large, the less the characters know, the more they'll get wrong and the more drama you'll generate. When writing the first draft the important thing is simply to release and not to edit.

Can you learn to write dialogue?

No. You either have an ear for it or you don't. Some people can impersonate others credibly, some can't. Some can remember *what* was said but never *how* it was said. Naturally, if you have a basic facility for writing dialogue, you can improve it. The way to do this is very simple and involves one word: listening. In normal conversation we get the gist of what the person is saying and move on quickly to think of how we are going to reply. It is important for the playwright not just to listen to *what* is being said, but also to get used to being aware of *how* it is being said.

Whilst it's fatal when writing dialogue to have your characters say exactly what they mean, in first drafts it is probably advantageous to write the play as though it were some kind of B-movie. The dialogue can be really cold and mundane but at least you know what the character wants, and what the scene is about. When you come to rewrite it for the second draft you will already know what is 'on the menu'. The best definition of what the playwright does for the theatre actor is: to give the actor something to *do*. Not something to *say*. That may sound paradoxical. By 'something to do' I don't mean that the actor crosses to the stage left and turns on the TV – that's not action, that's business. Action is dependent on goals and upon characters needing to achieve something. It is the combination of what they want to achieve and the way they go about achieving it that makes their character and creates subtext.

If I ask an actor to improvise a scene where they enter a room and see another character present, the odds are, unless they are brilliant improvisers, the scene will fall completely flat. But if I say to the actor entering the room, 'You want to con the other character into lending you money', then some dramatic action will occur. The other character will be forced to make a decision: to give up some money or not. If I add a third ingredient – that the character doing the conning is nervous – then not only will action occur but character will develop as they pursue their goal. Subtext will be created and, with it, good dialogue. Similarly, the other characters will emerge in the way they react to our con man; are they taken in or do they play along out of kindness? In a sense the key to writing good dialogue is to deny your characters the knowledge you have about their desires, to not let them know what it is they need most of all in the story or how they are going to achieve it. Give your characters simple objectives one at a time, and a complex pattern will emerge. Do not overburden them with information. You cannot write all of the play all of the time.

A word of warning

The commonest mistake that playwrights make is the failure to put the characters under pressure to make decisions. I have read plays in which the writer desperately wants their audience to care about the plight of their central character – be they redundant steelworkers or oppressed women – but has achieved exactly the opposite because he or she has failed to send the character 'into battle'. It is fine, perhaps, for the first ten minutes or so of your play to be about the 'still pond' the characters' lives have become, but it cannot go on endlessly. The protagonist must face a challenge and embrace it. How many times have you seen a play in which the central character is immobile, trapped in a narrative that fails to develop and so is compelled to do nothing other than bemoan their lot?

Empathy is generated when characters take risks. It is easy to fall into the trap of making the protagonist reactive (the victim of forces surrounding them) rather than active (taking decisions under pressure which initiate change). I think the reason for this is that when we look at our own lives we often feel like victims, forced to carry out sometimes quite unappealing tasks by those around us or by the world in general. But look back on your life objectively and you will see that, whilst pressure will have been placed on you by others, you will also have made many choices, taken many decisions, taken risks. Even the refusal to take a decision is in itself risky and dangerous because it brings with it the possibility of missing the boat. In all our lives, the mortality clock is ticking in the background. Human beings want to avoid change, but change we must and change we do. In real life, change takes months or even years. The playwright does not have the luxury of that time, so your job is to compress the process of change so that an audience sense they have seen a complete life journey in the ninety-minute traffic that is your play.

In Willy Russell's *Shirley Valentine*, it takes Shirley some considerable time to pluck up the courage to go on holiday with her friend, to go 'into battle'. But once she does, the play then enters its most interesting and challenging phase for both Shirley and her audience. It's already been discussed that this is the inciting incident, the moment without which the play would not happen. Take away this vital moment or incident and there would be no story. What is the irreversible moment in your play when the little snowball is pushed off the mountain, gathering speed and later causing an avalanche?

The climax of a play is always an answer to the 'What happens if . . . ?' posed by the inciting incident. In *Shirley Valentine*, we see what happens if a woman trapped in a dull and lifeless marriage risks going on holiday with her friend without her husband's consent. She finds her own voice.

Now you must find yours . . .

PART TWO

Getting to the End

Keep your head

The hardest thing for any writer, far harder than creating character, plot and structure, is getting to the end. It requires a colossal amount of both self-belief and self-delusion.

Remember how Ibsen observed that, over the course of three drafts, his characters progressed from being as familiar to him as fellow train passengers to being like people he had known all his life. Console yourself with the fact that it's natural to struggle your way through the first draft, knowing full well that characters are speaking in a way you hate, mouthing the plot, and inhabiting a wobbly structure with predictable plot twists. The purpose of the first draft is simply to fill the pages. Get to the end. Set yourself a target of a certain number of pages per day and write them regardless. And, above all else, do not go back and start to revise. There is no point in revising Scene One until you have finished the play, because as a writer you will not know what needs to be in the first scene until you have written the final one. I have wasted endless hours – and have come across hundreds of other writers who have done the same – simply rewriting Scenes One, Two, Three . . .

Do not begin the day by looking back over what you wrote yesterday. If you can't remember what you have written, perhaps you don't care enough about the subject or are treating the creation of a work of art in too academic a way. You must know roughly what happened, so keep on moving forwards. You are playing a psychological trick on yourself to give yourself the feeling of momentum, which is the most crucial thing. Don't get caught by the feeling of being stuck on a play and having to drag yourself to the computer every morning to start typing again when everything inside you is screaming, 'No, no, no!'

That's why it is important that, firstly, you just fill the pages and, lastly, you know when to stop filling the pages. Do not stop writing when you have reached a block. Try and compel yourself to stop when you are on a high. Stop when you know what the characters are going to say next. Stop when you are excited about the next scene. Now this is quite hard to do because you are probably suffering from the myth that you are in the middle of a great creative rush and you must carry on. Well, do it if you must, but there is the risk that you will write yourself out, and find it incredibly difficult the next day to come back to the play. And this is where, I think, the dreadful phrase 'writer's block' comes from. I don't believe it is a genuine psychological condition. It is a crisis of faith. You have got to tell yourself that every playwright goes through this. The first draft is like pulling teeth.

Keep on keeping on

Once you start to write, you will be fired up with the adrenaline rush that the release of creativity brings. It's like falling in love with someone: everything is perfect, and life is transformed. But then you will probably hit a wall after about fifteen to twenty pages when suddenly you start to think, 'Where am I? What's the story?' – and you will be tempted to go back to the beginning. And in that temptation to go back – convincing yourself that you are simply re-familiarising yourself with the material – you will get bogged down in your own failure. You will start to fiddle with sentence structure or start to move commas. In short, you will start doing anything that avoids going forwards into the unknown, because the unknown fills you with fear. You will have become a passive protagonist in your own drama. You will have failed to send yourself into action. You have got to keep moving forwards. A key to this is keeping in mind the backbone of the story and sticking to it. Arthur Miller used to stick a single sentence on his typewriter to remind him, in narrative terms, what the play was about. For *Death of a Salesman*, for example, something like: 'This is the story of a man who cannot accept that his days as a salesman are over.'

The crucial thing is to keep the play in focus at some time during each day. Even if you can only work on it for one, five or thirty minutes a day, keep the rhythm going. The moment you get out of the habit of writing every day (for however short a time), and real life intervenes, it is amazing how quickly your project will disappear from view and the subconscious will cease to work on it. Everyone can find twenty minutes in their day to work: do it.

Getting stuck

It's not a question of 'if', but 'when'. You *will* get stuck. Most of this 'stuckness' will be caused by self-doubt, by the fear that you are not good enough. Well, in all probability you aren't good enough. But then again neither is anyone else. Fail, fail again, and fail better. All works of art are flawed, all stories imperfect, all narrative imprecise. Once you have that idea in your head, the fear of failure will leave you for ever. Do not be the sort of writer for whom the band is playing in the other room. If you do get stuck on a specific scene then leap forwards. Just keep on writing.

When your creative juices dry up it's sometimes best to walk away from the play. Find diversionary tactics: take the dog for a walk, go for a swim, bake a cake, masturbate. Do something that engages other aspects of your brain. This often allows the creative juices to flow, whereas sitting at your desk metaphorically (or maybe literally) beating your head against the computer screen seldom produces anything. Of course to go off and walk the dog or bake a cake will feel like an avoidance tactic, and sometimes it will be. But eighty per cent of the work of the writer is not done at the desk. I would even suggest that thirty or forty per cent is not even done consciously. When the play is in focus it is something that happens in the deep subconscious.

Getting stuck in

I would suggest you hold off the moment you begin to write for as long as you can bear to let your ideas ferment in your mind, but don't hold off too long. Don't simply avoid work. To paraphrase Quentin Crisp: 'After eight weeks your day-dreams may start to become an alibi.' The time spent before you start to write is akin to being pregnant: you will know when your waters are breaking and you need to give birth.

At this point, begin to write in any way you want: in pencil, in pen, on the computer, on a beer mat, at home, in a café, in the bath, on the bus or on the train. Wherever. Find the situation and the circumstances that work for you. Many people say, 'I haven't time to write a play.' It doesn't take that long. A play isn't a novel; it doesn't have that many words in it. You always find time for what you really want to do. (So if you can't find the time doesn't that call into question how much you want to be a writer?)

Imagine if you were to set aside half an hour every day; maybe half an hour on the bus on the way to work, half an hour before the kids come home from school, set your alarm clock half an hour earlier in the morning. Imagine, if you did this every day, how much you would achieve in a month. Every journey begins with a first step. The important thing is to keep moving forwards, not to go back, not to edit and not to censor, but to *release.*

You must accept that in your first draft your characters will be in some sense like strangers to you. But this very process is, in part, about getting to know them, how they walk, talk, think and feel, and it is about getting them to speak to you. Treat your first draft as though it were a lump of rock and you were a sculptor. To start with, you are simply knocking away the rough edges, getting the vague outline of the people and their world. It is no good spending hours and hours carving out the most perfectly formed feet because you may find that by the time you finish your statue this character is a double amputee. Just get a rough shape.

Above all, try and keep relaxed. Tension is the death of creativity. The tension that drives you to write is fine, but once you start to write, it is vital that you relax. Don't punish yourself. Don't fear failure. Do enjoy yourself – remember the word for what you're creating is 'play'. Just keep in mind that this is simply the first draft and that the chief object is to fill the pages. To get to the end.

Some questions

The next stage is all down to you, and I would suggest you put this book down and simply enjoy doing some writing! However, if you get stuck or lack inspiration, the following prompt questions might help you work through some obstacles that are hindering you getting to the end.

How much exposition do you need at the start?

I would say as little as possible. Gone are the days when the audience needed or wanted a whole act to get to know the characters. Nowadays we are far happier being plunged straight into the fray with exposition turned into ammunition.

Take, for example, the opening scene of Joe Penhall's *Love and Understanding*. The lights come up on a living room in London. We hear a plane overhead. Neal says, 'We're under the flight path. One every two minutes.' Richie replies, 'Very nice. All yours?' Neal: 'Will be one day.' Richie: 'I'm impressed.' From these four very simple lines we learn so much.

We learn it is Neal's house. We learn that he and Richie have a past. We learn Richie has not been to the house before and because of the tension between the two characters we get an instant sense that Neal feels under pressure from the unexpected arrival of his old friend. In just four lines the play is up and running. Richie is driving the scene as he attempts to pressure Neal into letting him stay the night. We sense Neal doesn't want him there but Neal's inability to say no (his inner conflict) combined with Richie's persistence means that Richie does stay, with shattering consequences for Neal and his girlfriend. In the original production Richie was played by Paul Bettany who, though a charmer, gave the audience an instant sense that the character was dangerous and that there was trouble on the horizon. What Penhall has done here is to convert the factual information he needs to convey (the exposition) into dramatically interesting things that the characters have to say to get what they want (the ammunition).

Invariably you will find that if you write the opening scene with the assumption that the audience already knows the facts about your characters' lives, then these facts will become apparent – and if they don't, the odds are that they're irrelevant. Do not try and hide information for the sake of cleverness but never underestimate an audience's ability or desire to deduce things for themselves. Let the action fill in the backstory organically. Remember the idea that characters only speak to get what they want. Let them reveal facts about themselves in the pursuit of their goals.

Do you have an inciting incident?

Without an inciting incident I suspect your play will fail to begin. In Joe Penhall's *Love and Understanding*, it is when Neal allows Richie to stay with him and his girlfriend. In *King Lear* it's the point where Lear banishes Cordelia. It's the moment the playwright poses an active question both for his characters and, by implication, the audience. It's the 'What happens if . . . ?' moment. It's the point where the protagonist embarks on a gamble and embraces the challenge set to him or her by the narrative. Never be afraid to simplify your story to a single sentence that clearly expresses this: 'What happens if a woman tries to escape an abusive relationship?' 'What happens if a man attempts to take over the family business?' It's not rocket science. Even small children know the basics of storytelling; they understand implicitly the 'What happens if . . . ?' principle.

Ideally you are looking for a sentence that anticipates the action and hints at the consequences of what the central character or characters are about to do. This line is not thematic or opaque; it's simple and practical. This will be the governing principle of your drama, the river from which all tributaries must flow, the journey on which you, your characters and your audience have now embarked. The best plays are complex, not necessarily complicated. No amount of tortuous plot twists can substitute for depth, and depth comes from telling a clear story well.

Remember that a character cannot win or lose all his money until he actually enters the casino. Ask yourself if your characters are simply standing outside the door of the casino or if you have pushed them inside? Your central character (or characters) must embrace *consciously* the challenge thrown down by the inciting incident and embark on a course of action. Do you know specifically what that challenge is and how they respond to it? Is the course of action they have embarked on dangerous? Does it involve risk – that they are aware of, or unaware of, or both?

In Catherine Johnson's play *Shang-a-Lang*, four women decide to go to a Bay City Roller's tribute weekend at Butlins. The inciting incident is the decision to go, leaving their normal lives and crossing into the uncharted territory of a weekend away from their husbands and boyfriends. Needless to say, none of them emerges from the weekend without their lives changed in some way. All good stories are in some sense a bet. 'What happens if a man decides to give away his kingdom?' (*King Lear*); 'What happens if a man cannot accept he no longer needs to sell to live?' (*Death of a Salesman*); 'What happens if a young woman goes against her domineering mother's wishes and develops a relationship with a man from the village?' (*The Beauty Queen of Leenane*); 'What happens if a man falls in love with a goat?' (*The Goat*). In your writing, complete the sentence, 'What happens if . . . ?' – and stick to it!

Now the bet is on. The gamble is undertaken. Your protagonist has made a decision under pressure. Excitement and anticipation are now in the air. You ask yourself what you would do in this situation. 'Playing God', you consider what would be best for your protagonist to do, and as an audience we watch as the character acts autonomously. We watch in awe as Lear banishes Cordelia from his court (in spite of the advice of those closest to him) and wait to see if our worst fears are confirmed.

[53]

Do your characters travel on a 'journey abroad'?

So you have set up your play, and your protagonist or protagonists have undertaken a gamble. They have embraced the challenge thrown down by the narrative. They are, metaphorically speaking, 'journeying abroad', playing away from home.

Think about this for a moment, for it will help you in the next stage of the story. Think about how you behave when you get to a new city in a foreign country. Think about how many idiotic mistakes you make in those first few days, how many dodgy restaurants you visit, how many wrong routes you take on the subway system. In short, how naive you are. The same must now be true of your central character/s. They are where they have not been before. They will err. They will take the wrong turnings. They will convince themselves the dodgy food is good because they are in a strange country and 'this is how it is meant to taste'. They will tell themselves they are having a better time than they really are because they are on holiday. After all, by embracing the challenge they have made the choice to come here and feel they ought to be having a good time. They will do anything but turn back for home and admit the decision they made to come here in the first place was wrong. To admit otherwise would be to admit they chose the wrong holiday destination (and though we have all done that, how many of us truly admit to it at the time?).

Instead, we tough it out, we make the best of it, we lie to ourselves and to those around us, or worse still, we enter profound denial. All these reactions are truthful to the 'human condition', and are fantastic fuel for your character and your narrative. Do not commit the cardinal sin of granting your protagonist too much self-knowledge at this stage in the story, otherwise they will sprint for the finish. It will kill the narrative and also make the character unappealing to an audience. Why should we care about someone who knows they are doing the wrong thing for themselves but continues regardless?

In John Schlesinger's film adaptation of James Leo Herlihy's novel *Midnight Cowboy*, Joe Buck doesn't know quite what he is doing when he walks out on his job in a small-town diner, dons cowboy gear and heads to New York to hustle 'a lot of lonely rich women'. His co-worker at the diner seems unconvinced by Joe's plan, but Joe (like Lear) is having none of it. We stick around to find out if our fears and those of his co-workers are confirmed. And crucially we stick around because Joe is a sympathetic character. And why is he sympathetic? Because we can see how naive he is, because his actions are born of the need to escape his past rather than simply to get rich, and, importantly, because he embraces a challenge ('making it' in New York). Then, having embraced the challenge thrown down by the story and committed himself to a course of action (leaving the world he knows), Joe has begun the journey to a new world, a territory he is unfamiliar with. A territory for which he has no map. New York is not just a place; it is a state of mind. How will Joe survive, both literally and psychologically?

We care when a character can't cope and loses control, such as the title character in David Mamet's *Edmond* or Danny, the soldier returning to Britain from Basra, in Simon Stephen's *Motortown*. You should make your characters strangers to themselves in a strange land. This will place them in danger, create suspense and empathy, and raise the temperature of your story. We care about those in danger who battle on, even if the forward momentum takes them in the wrong direction. In their pursuit of something, their actions mirror our own daily struggles.

Are your characters 'coming across'?

I often panic about this when I get ten or fifteen pages into a play. I fear that the action I have written does not explain enough about the people concerned. I fear I have been too frugal in my exposition. I fear the audience don't know enough about my characters to care about them. If the characters are pursuing goals and doing it in a way that is different from how anyone else in the play would do it then you have created 'character in action'. Let them reveal the truth about themselves to you rather than the other way around. It seems to me a more organic approach, and one more likely to yield surprises that avoid 'off the peg' characterisation and stereo-typical behaviour. The characters will tell you who they are, not by what they *say*, but by what they *do* and the way in which they do it. No matter what accent you give them, no matter how you dress them, no matter what age you make them, character cannot emerge without goals and the pursuit of those goals. So keep them driving on and listen to them.

Some vital elements

Cause and effect

So your character has begun a journey, reacted to the inciting incident, made a decision under pressure and embarked on a course of action. You have lift off. Having embraced the chal-lenge, your protagonist has entered territory that he or she has not been in before, either literally or metaphorically. Territory for which they have no map and in which they do not know the rules. In your story, return again to your protagonist and to his or her psychological state.

Work out the 'causal logic' of the drama. In moving forwards you are always dealing with cause and effect; every action leads to a reaction and, in turn, further action: action . . . reaction . . . action. It is just how it is in life, except in life it may take us months to make a decision. Make sure the decisions your characters take are logical, based on what we know about them thus far. If you fail in this the audience's trust in you will break down. Cause and effect is crucial. Every action creates a reaction and pushes the story forwards in an organic way.

Gaps between scenes

The gaps between scenes can be as crucial as the scenes them-selves, and you need to know what happened to your char-acters even when the audience were unable to see them. In film, as in the novel, it is possible to show every beat as it hap-pens, changing location in an instant, the raise of an eyebrow conveying a whole hinterland of psychology. Theatre is a different beast and whilst we, as an audience, want to sense that we have experienced every beat of your story, we do not necessarily want to see ten scenes in ten different locations of one line each.

Allowing a time gap between scenes also allows you to deploy another tool in the playwright's cupboard: surprise. Imagine two scenes, A and B. If, in Scene B, your characters' circumstances are considerably different from what they were in Scene A, the audience will sit up and take notice: what exactly is going on here? It may be a little while before they realise that time has elapsed between the scenes, and they will have to work hard to catch up. Handled properly, this can be to your advantage. It's a technique that John Osborne employs in Act Three of *Look Back in Anger* when suddenly it's Helena at the ironing board previously occupied by Alison. The audience, as soon as they realise that time has elapsed, are busy working out what has happened in the intervening period. They will enjoy filling in the gaps, as long as you make sure you take them with you. They don't want to be left in the dark, anxious that they've missed something, but they do want to be challenged. They like to be active participants. And most of all, they like to feel confident that you the writer know exactly what you're doing.

However, a note of caution. Time gaps like this often lead the playwright to write the following scene as if it's the first scene of the play, with lots of expositional, gap-filling dialogue along the lines of 'Wasn't it nice that day we went to Blackpool and you told me you loved me?' Forget this. As long as you know what has happened in the intervening period – and you do need to know, even if you write the scenes but never use them – the audience will get it. You won't have to make it explicit. It will be implicit in the scene, just as when you overhear a couple talking in a restaurant about their meal and can very quickly deduce the state of their relationship and the mood they are in. If *you* know, your audience will know.

The first-act climax

I've read many plays which fail to reach a moment of climax in the first act, and the protagonist remains trapped in the first phase of the story. You must keep driving your protagonist on so that they reach a point of major change, otherwise your audience will get frustrated at the lack of narrative development and the heat will go out of the drama. The first-act climax is an exciting and important point in your storytelling. Your protagonist has reached the end of the line on the journey you triggered in the inciting incident and is forced to embark on a new course of action.

In David Frankel's film *The Devil Wears Prada*, based on Lauren Weisberger's novel of the same name, the first-act climax occurs when the protagonist decides to fully embrace the value system of the fashion magazine where she works, a complete volte-face from her position at the start of the story. This is the point where metaphorically you have got your character/s 'up a tree'. They have committed to a course of action which the audience senses will ultimately cause them big problems. In *The Devil Wears Prada*, we sense that the protagonist has agreed to betray herself, and we stick around to find out what the consequences of that will be.

Complication

So your protagonist is up a tree. The crucial thing about this stage of the story is that (a) the protagonist commits fully to their new course of action and (b) that it presents a logical and apparent solution to their dilemma after the inciting incident. In other words, it feels inevitable and organic. You are now ready to throw stones at the character. If you don't, then you will not bring them face to face with the truth about themselves. Lear has to be rejected by both Goneril and Regan in order to end up on the heath with Poor Tom and to learn the truth about himself. This rejection by his daughters then forms the action of the second act of *King Lear* (although the play is structured in five acts, it is actually written as a three-act play in narrative terms).

Such complications are useful but dangerous things. I have been trying to encourage you, whilst recognising the basic tenets of storytelling (beginning–middle–end), to let your protagonist drive your narrative. Complication, if inorganic, can be the theatrical equivalent of a hand grenade lobbed into the centre of the narrative, exploding with a force that destroys the crafted structure you are creating. An example of an effective complication is Harper finding out he's HIV positive in *Angels in America* by Tony Kushner; a diagnosis that comes out of the blue but is totally thematically consistent.

Complications keep the pressure on the central character and cause the story to escalate. But be sure to make your complications organic and that they further develop the narrative journey you embarked upon in the inciting incident of your story, otherwise you will be effectively starting a whole new play in the second act!

Escalation

Escalation is another important tool for the storyteller and most great stories employ it. In drama, escalation occurs from the moment the curtain rises, and the speed of the escalation will tend to increase as the story goes on. It's interesting to note that both farce and tragedy use this technique but with quite different results in terms of the feelings they evoke in the audience. The stakes should rise for your characters. The risk they took in the inciting incident of the story may have been minimal – it may not have seemed like a risk at all – but in the second act of the story (or perhaps earlier), we will begin to see the full implications of the gamble undertaken.

Returning to the analogy of your central character entering a casino and placing a bet, by this stage in your narrative the odds against them winning are getting higher and higher. The more they risk, the more hopeless their situation, the more drawn to them we are. Imagine you were a spectator in an actual casino. Which table would you be drawn to watching? The one where a person places small, sensible, regular bets or the one where they risk everything in their wallet and their lover looks on, horrified? Drama cannot be ordinary people in ordinary circumstances. We get that at home!

The second-act climax

Like the first-act climax, this represents a major turning point for the central character. Often it is a turning point which leads to an action that is diametrically opposed to the one they took at the end of Act One. In *Shadowlands*, C.S. Lewis opted to love at the end of Act One. Now, at the end of Act Two, that love, in the form of a woman who seemingly provided the answers to all his problems, is taken away from him by cancer. He feels worse than he did at the start of the story. He may even wish he had never met her, as we all do in the immediate aftermath of a painful break-up. The story has been turned on its head.

Having begun the story as a omnipotent monarch, Lear ends the first act as a man who has power with no responsibility. At the end of the second act, he has no power, no responsibility and no clothes; he's reduced to the level of a beggar. If you are writing in a three-act form, the second-act climax is the point at which your character is propelled towards the crisis of the story.

Crisis

Crisis is a frequently misused term. It's not whether or not to jump off a burning building into the arms of a fireman. It's not a clear-cut, black-and-white decision. If in the 'crisis moment', a character has to simply choose between safety and danger, that's not a genuine crisis. A crisis is a difficult decision requiring courage, created by the story, and offering gain as well as pain. For example, Othello has to choose between living with the agony of having been betrayed, or ending his own life and at least escaping the pain of this world.

In Willy Russell's *Shirley Valentine,* the crisis point comes for Shirley when she receives a letter from her husband asking her to go back home to her family. She has to choose between her own happiness and that of her family. She opts to stay in Greece, but Russell then layers the ending by allowing her husband to come and see her. Thus the ending is not black and white; we are left wondering what will happen. It shows that Shirley has changed, found her own voice and developed the strength to stand up to her abusive husband – but also that perhaps he has changed too. We never know what happens when he comes to meet her. However, the meeting will be on her terms and not his – which represents a seismic shift in her relationship with him, with herself and with the world around her. The crisis leads organically to the climax.

Climax

Put quite simply, the climax is the result of the decision taken by the protagonist at the moment of crisis. If, in the inciting incident of your story, your protagonist began an extra-marital affair, then the crisis probably involved he or she being brought face to face with the full consequences and having to make a decision (staying in an unsatisfactory marriage for the sake of the kids versus leaving and losing them) and the climax is the outcome after making their decision. If the crisis is 'the day of reckoning', then the climax is the day after!

Many playwrights struggle massively with the climax of their plays, and well they might – because the opening and the ending are by far the most important sections of the play. Fail to hook the audience in the first three minutes, and it's game over. Fail to send them out with a cracking ending and all your good work will be undermined. Any stand-up comedian will tell you that the place to put the dodgy material is in the middle. Begin with a bang – and end with bang.

Ultimately, the ending will depend on your worldview. Are you an optimist? Are you a pessimist? Are you a bit of both? As with all of this, the answer is to be honest and to excavate psychological territory that only you know.

Resolution

This is where the underlying meaning of the story is converted into action. The key word here is 'action'. In drama, actions speak louder than words. Who can remember a line of dialogue from *A Doll's House*? And yet who can forget what the protagonist Nora does at the end of the play when she slams the door on her husband and her life? This action occurs in the final moments after the crisis in which Nora is brought face to face with the consequences of borrowing money behind her husband's back and, perhaps more importantly, with the reality of her situation as a woman.

Good endings are often shaded grey areas. They provide more questions than answers. Yes, they answer the narrative question posed at the beginning of the story, but they should also make the audience question their own lives and assumptions. In a tragedy like *King Lear* the man has lost everything, the kingdom and the daughter he loves, but the earth is razed. Everything is cleared. The old order has gone. There is a sense of renewal in the kingdom. For Lear the game is up, but for the audience there is a sense that life can begin again. All great tragedies provide you with the sense that everything has been stripped bare and that we can rebuild.

The end of your play is where you will send out a message to the audience. Not necessarily a tub-thumping, campaigning proclamation, but a message none the less. Remember, you set up this story. You posed an active question in the inciting incident – 'What happens if . . . ?' – and this is effectively the answer you are sending the audience away with. Ask yourself: 'Am I happy with it? Is it challenging or reactionary? Is it shaded or simplistic? Importantly, is it how my story really should end? Is it the story only I know?'

The first draft

By this stage – after tears and torment, alcoholism and excessive procrastination, after treating those you love with disdain and disrespect, behaving abominably to your mother and repeatedly kicking the cat – you have arrived at the end of something approaching a first draft. It may be in order, it may not. But whatever you do with it now, I would suggest you go away and find something to occupy your time because you are no use to this story at present. You've taken a solid piece of marble, and you have hacked out a very rough shape of what you want. The fine detail is not there yet; the eyes and the nose are not specific or defined enough. We cannot, perhaps, even make out who it is. But we don't need to at this point.

This is the perfect opportunity to indulge yourself and importantly, I think, to interact with other people. It can't be underestimated how crucial it is for the writer to remain connected to the real world. It is very easy, particularly as your career progresses as a playwright, to spend increasing amounts of your time around fellow 'theatre people', directors and actors. This is fine, but you must also remain in touch with the world beyond. Perhaps having finished the first draft you have to return to work, or you have to get a job in order to fund the next stage of your writing, in which case I suggest you take a job which demands you use a completely different section of your brain, or in which you might actually garner material for a future play. Nothing excites literary managers and artistic directors more than a writer who has written from experience, a writer who has actually *been* there.

*

The period away from the play should be long enough for you to be surprised when you return to it. What you are attempting to do is place yourself in the position of the audience or reader, to view your work with objectivity. When you do return to it I suggest you find yourself a nice, relaxing situation and read your script, without making notes, without crossing out, without underlining. This is a very 'broad brushstroke' reading. The aim in writing the second draft should not be to polish lines and sentence structure: that comes later. You are now about to embark on the stage Ibsen likened to spending a long weekend with your characters, so getting an overview of what you have created thus far is vital.

I would certainly ask other people to read the play at this stage as well. But those people would be very close to me, people I trusted and had worked with over many years. People whose views I respected and who understood where I was coming from, not just as a writer but also as a human being. You shouldn't be looking to show your first draft to literary managers or artistic directors or to anybody connected with any theatre to which you may eventually send the play (unless you have an established developmental relationship with them). The temptation is to send the play out too early. Time and time again when I was a literary manager I'd receive scripts from people saying, 'I've written the first draft. I know it's not right but maybe you could give me some feedback to get me started on the second draft.' Well, if it is an absolutely brilliant first draft that may have been a good move by the playwright – but nine times out of ten I would be put off ever wanting to read that play again. As a chef you wouldn't serve a half-prepared meal in a restaurant. You must not send your script out half-dressed in public, or you will find it coming home in tears.

The other thing you could consider at this stage is whether you would like to hear the first draft read out loud. If so, then I would suggest you recruit some friends or actors. But do not, under any circumstances, stage this reading in front of an audience. The reason for this is that the actors will simply try to produce a 'performance' of your play; good actors, in particular, are very capable at a reading of hiding the faults in a script. This could well give you a false sense of security about the play, convincing you that there is less work to do than you think. Similarly, if you workshop the play with very poor actors in front of an audience, this may crush your confidence. On the other hand, a private reading, whatever the calibre of the actors, gives you some sense of what the play might sound like on its feet. Some sense of the muscularity of the piece. It will also give you a sense of the sections that drag, or are repetitive, or where the narrative fails to move forwards. If you can't get hold of actors, try reading the draft yourself into a tape recorder. You will soon get a clear picture of the sections which drag and the speeches which do not belong.

As you read your first draft – or listen to it read aloud – there will be bits you like. If you are lucky, there will be lots that you like, but more likely there will be chunks that you absolutely hate and can't believe that you could ever have written. Well, as I said before, you have to put these to one side in your mind and not let them drag you down. All writers feel they have failed in some way with a play: it is part and parcel of being a good writer. As Ernest Hemingway said, 'The first draft of anything is shit.'

Questions to ask yourself

As you read your first draft (and, for that matter, any draft of your play), you should be constantly considering the following questions:

▸ What's the story?

▸ Who is the protagonist?

▸ What does he or she want in any scene?

▸ What does he or she want at the start of the play?

▸ What does he or she want at the end of the play?

▸ How different is the character at the end from the character at the start?

▸ Has a change been forced upon them, or did they simply choose to make it themselves?

▸ Did the narrative continually place them under pressure?

▸ How long did it take for my story to kick off?

▸ What is the bet or the risk that the protagonist takes?

▸ And what is the result of that risk in the climactic moment of the drama?

▸ Is there a first-act climax? What is it?

▸ Is there a second-act climax? What is it?

▶ Is there a third-act climax? What is it?

▶ If I was to remove my characters from the play and place them in any situation (i.e. asking someone out, getting on a bus, ordering food in a restaurant) would I know how they would do it? Could I improvise that dialogue instantly?

▶ What are the levels of conflict in my play? The extra-personal level, the inter-personal level and, crucially, the inner level?

▶ In what ways are my characters their own worst enemies?

▶ Are my characters simply victims of other people and the story?

▶ Can I hear my characters? If I cover up the names of them in the script, can I tell who is saying what?

▶ Are my locations interesting? Do they offer contrast from one scene to another? Do they create different atmospheres? Do they place the characters in different arenas? How do these contexts affect their relationships with others and with themselves?

▶ Do I know why I am writing the next draft? Are there simple, specific things I am trying to achieve?

▶ Am I trying to write all of the play all of the time (i.e. put everything into every scene, destroying any sense of reality)?

The story

In considering all these questions as you read your first draft, there's one thing that you should be concentrating on. To paraphrase Bill Clinton: 'It's the story, stupid.' What is your story? Having read the script, can you write it on the back of a matchbox, which is where all good stories ought to fit: 'There was a man who . . . '; 'This is the story of when a woman . . . '; 'What happens if a man does . . . ' Go back to the very basic storytelling techniques so that you have a very clear idea of the story you are trying to tell – and what you have so far told. The space between these two stories is where the work needs to be done in the second draft.

At this stage it may be useful for you to clarify the story as it currently exists. Break the play down into scenes and write each scene heading on a postcard, along with the main action of the scene, expressed in very broad brushstrokes. For instance, 'Scene One. The Palace. Lear decides to divide up his kingdom. He invites his daughters to tell him how much they love him. Cordelia does not give him what he wants. He banishes her from his kingdom.' Or 'Scene One: Richie arrives at Neal's house unexpectedly and persuades Neal to let him stay.' Clarity and simplicity are the keys, for when you come to write the second draft, the simpler the story seems at any given point, the more chance you have of creating dialogue and character that truly comes alive. There is nothing worse than a writer using six- or seven-tenths of their brain to focus on the plot, the themes and the overall arc, only to find themselves crippled by being unable to improvise the dialogue.

Let's say that in Scene One of your play, X enters and wants to ask Y out; Y wants to go out with X, but X is scared to ask. That's all you need to know to kick off a scene. Character X has an objective; he also has the requisite inner conflict (he is too shy to ask); he has a person towards whom he can act, with whom he can attempt to achieve his goal. Remember the definition of a scene: 'A unit of action in which something changes.' Examine your scenes. Does something or someone change in each of them?

Having encapsulated each of your scenes on postcards and laid them out, you might want to change the order around. What happens if Scene Three comes before Scene Two? What happens if the play begins at Scene Five? It is important to keep all your options open. You must still be willing to ask yourself the big questions about whether a character is actually required, if the narrative is going in the right direction, or if you really need that plot strand or sequence of scenes. You need to put into practice the objective opinions and decision-making that you would exercise on someone else's work. It is the hardest thing in the world to do, and you won't achieve it a hundred per cent, but the bolder, the braver and the less precious you are, the more chance you have of ultimately delivering a successful play.

The characters

As you read your first draft, see if it is clear what your characters are trying to achieve in each and every scene. What are their goals? What are the obstacles that prevent them achieving those goals? Be certain that at all times characters are pursuing goals, both conscious and unconscious. David Mamet's observation, that people only speak to get what they want, is pertinent. Are your characters trying to get things or are they merely telling each other things they already know? This is a common problem in first drafts: the author, anxious to communicate facts about the story to the audience and nervous of not making things clear, forces his characters to mouth the plot. Do not be embarrassed if you do this. It's far better that the first draft be overwritten than undercooked, since it's easier to 'bury' intentions in the second draft than excavate them.

You might find it useful to ask someone to read out all of one character's lines in order and in isolation from the other characters. This enables you to get a clearer sense of whether or not each individual character develops and where the moments of change occur. Where are the turning points? How well are they realised? Do you herd your characters through gates, or do the choices they make seem perfectly in keeping with their personalities? This exercise can be a very immediate — and often funny — way of exposing characters who, in developmental terms, are endlessly stuck in a rut, mouthing the same thing in different ways. Character is decision under pressure. Character should be in constant evolution. Character should always be journeying towards or away from itself; sometimes both, but never neither. Evolution is all.

Other – more subsidiary – characters can have the same complexity as the central character but must be built to feed into the protagonist's journey which remains the play's focus. If these subsidiary characters are not created to interact with the main story there's a danger that the audience will not know who the play is actually about or will feel that you as a writer have 'changed lanes' halfway through the story. Are your subsidiary characters feeding into the main narrative or hijacking it? Do you find yourself more interested in a subsidiary character and want to focus on them as the protagonist in the next draft? If so, this is almost like beginning a new play but may be an important part of your process.

The dialogue

At this stage you should not be too worried about the minutiae of your dialogue. You should be thinking about the overall arc and architecture of the piece. Will the building still stand up – and what work needs to be done if it won't, so that it is in a fit state to unveil in front of an audience? It may be that when you come to write your second draft you merely take the action, the goals and the obstacles that you identified when writing the first draft, and completely rewrite the dialogue. Maybe writing the first draft was merely a way of familiarising yourself with the characters and now you can write dialogue for them with much fuller understanding.

When looking at your dialogue, be aware of subtext that you weren't aware of creating. Alan Bennett has talked of reading one of his own plays and suddenly discovering things in his 'suitcase' that he didn't remember packing. It may be that in these unexpected items you will find the key to your story, or something that propels you into the second draft. Perhaps you will just see the tip of the iceberg of the play that you are trying to write, as opposed to the one that you have so far written.

At this early stage, do not get too attached to any of your dialogue, single lines, purple passages or jokes. Joe Orton said that when a joke made him laugh out loud as he wrote it, he was pretty certain it would be cut in the next draft. You have to be tough with yourself and willing to 'slaughter your children'. Good plays aren't written, they're rewritten.

The second draft

During and after your reading of the first draft you must think about an approach for the second draft and what you must achieve with it. Is your task to think about the characters, or the locations? Minimising them, maximising them, varying them? Is your task to think about the structure, the narrative, the plotting? At this stage I often find doodles and diagrams can help; anything that encourages clear thinking and forces you to take an overview rather than getting caught up in too much detail. Some writers lay out a model of their story on the living-room floor, using objects representing key moments in the story or turning points for the characters. Others apportion a piece of music to the mood of a scene or give their scenes headings, e.g. 'The scene where X leaves Y' or 'The scene in which A crushes B's confidence'.

One thing I always try to avoid is writing the second draft with the first one next to me, and will generally put it totally to one side. I believe that any passage that is any good will come back to me, and what gets forgotten should probably stay forgotten. More importantly, though, this allows you to write your second draft with freedom. Imagine a friend of yours giving you a script that they were stuck on and saying, 'I've written a first draft; maybe you could write a second?' This is the relationship you should have with your own first draft. The more impartial you can be and the more you can place yourself in the position of the audience, the more you will be able to see the wood for the trees. The less you get wrapped up in the minutiae, the more chance you have of writing a better second draft.

So off you go to write the second draft. You no longer have to begin at the beginning and end at the end. You can write the scenes again in whichever order you want. But you should find that, because you know why the characters are entering a scene and what they are trying to achieve, the dialogue should start to flow more freely. Again, do not restrict yourself, do not wear a self-imposed straitjacket; let the characters and their dialogue run free. Remember that the less self-knowledge and awareness they have of the story they are in, the more they will come alive as 'real people' and the greater their journey will be. If you are a writer who rigidly planned your story before you started to write, now is the time to let your characters go 'off message', particularly if you think your play is too short. Let the characters range around, let them be themselves, free from the constraints of your planning. If you are the sort of writer who didn't plan before beginning to write and now find yourself with 180 pages of what should be a ninety-page script, then the opposite is probably true, and it is time to put your characters back 'on message'. Make them stick to the backbone of your narrative and cut away what is extraneous.

Above all, enjoy it. The more pleasure you get from the writing, the more the audience will enjoy the viewing and the director and actors will enjoy interpreting it. Do not substitute complication for complexity. Great plays do not require oodles and oodles of plot (unless, of course, you are attempting some Agatha Christie-like thriller or an intricate farce). Great plays are often simple but complex. Try to be tough with yourself and use your first draft as a springboard to your second draft rather than a template to be fiddled with.

*

Once you have reached the end of the second draft the same rules apply as at the first-draft stage: put the thing away and go and do something else. Now it might be at this stage that you decide to read around the play. You might choose to read up on aspects of history or politics, philosophy or science that you think may intersect in some way with your play. You may be the sort of writer who did this in your preliminary research, in which case maybe it's time to return to some of that? Maybe you are now much clearer about the genre of your play and you decide to read other successful examples of that genre – though be careful here, it's very easy inadvertently to copy plays you read whilst writing.

When you return to your play again, it is the same as when you returned to the first draft: you want to return with as clear a head and as much objectivity as possible. By now your characters should be approaching that second phase Ibsen described: they should be as familiar to you as people with whom you spent a long weekend in a country house but did not previously know.

The third draft

When you come back to analyse the second draft before beginning the third draft, all the same rules and considerations should come into play, and you might want to refer again to the earlier checklist of questions to ask yourself.

You may choose to ask trusted friends to read your second draft and offer feedback. You may think you are at a stage at which the play is ready to be sent out to theatres, producers and agents, but you will still require another draft (at least). All these notions of drafts and the number required are completely subjective, of course, but ponder what Ibsen said and ask yourself if your characters now speak like people you've known your whole life or is there more work to do? The third draft, if you are lucky, will not involve major surgery. It is rather about tightening up your work so far, dotting the 'i's and crossing the 't's.

When I write, by this stage I am beginning to pay particular attention to not just the structure and story arc, but also to the quality of the individual scenes and the dialogue. Early on it can be crippling, particularly in the first draft, to try and concentrate too much on the dialogue; you'll end up honing beautifully written scenes that may not ultimately be required for the play (and because they are 'beautifully written' you may have more difficulty jettisoning them). As I've said, it can be better to write those scenes quickly, even scrappily and in explicit terms.

When you start your third draft you should be looking to bury what is explicit and make the characters sound as much like real people as possible, rather than mouthpieces for your drama. Identify areas where your characters are mouthing the plot or have too great an awareness of the story they are in. As with your analysis of the first draft, you should be looking to identify all the major turning points in the story, but now your task may be to disguise them a little, so the audience cannot see them coming and (unless you want them to) the characters cannot see them coming. Your task when writing your third draft will be to make sure the audience cannot see the mechanism of the clock, merely its beautiful face. You want to make the play look effortless, the dialogue utterly natural, with scenes in which the characters behave exactly as they would in 'real life', in order that the audience never once question their suspension of disbelief. You are approaching the stage at which your play ought to begin to have an inevitability about it; a sense in which it could not happen in any other way.

*

If you find a scene is still not working despite having clear objectives, it may be that too many of your characters have a similar status within that scene. Equal status often leads to inertia and lack of drama. What you should be finding and showing is uneven status and reversals of status within the scene. Imagine the scene as a cardiographic chart showing the beating of a heart. It should not show a steady rhythm, but should fluctuate, sometimes alarmingly and unexpectedly, with the pulses switching organically throughout the scene.

Next, imagine you are in a rehearsal room, asking a group of actors to improvise the scene. What are the instructions you would give to each character? What are their objectives within the scene? Are the objectives different? Would these instructions allow the actors to improvise a dynamic and dramatic scene, or would they simply be forced to mouth the plot to each other? Often when a scene is not working it is because characters are *talking about* emotion rather than *generating* it. It is action, the pursuit of a goal and the success or failure to achieve that goal that generates emotion. Only a bad actor will play feelings; only a lazy writer will write them. You need to concentrate on the actions, what the characters do, and then the emotions will flow.

Imagine the opening scene of *King Lear* written as a bad TV movie. When Cordelia fails to tell Lear what he wants to hear, instead of banishing her from court he'd pour his heart out to Gloucester and say how disappointed he is in his prettiest daughter before nipping off for a counselling session. In actual fact, Shakespeare makes him bury that disappointment because of his pride, and convert it into anger, thus driving on the plot and creating subtext: we sense his disappointment even when he is being cruel to her. One of the best ways of generating subtext is to deny your characters self-knowledge: to make them their own worst enemies.

Are all your scenes 'active'? Is there something for the actors to do, not just say? Take a scene in which a girl woos and a boy succumbs. This can be expressed in ten lines or a hundred and ten depending on the characters and your writing style. It can be done in words or, for that matter, in silence, and the audience will still know what is going on. Why? Because you have given your characters clear goals and obstacles to the fulfilment of those goals, both internal and external. The dialogue can therefore take a myriad of forms. It can be straightforward naturalism; it can be heightened and poetic; it can be staccato and Pinteresque; the scene could even be played out in silence as a dumb show, but you will still be engaging the audience and telling the story only you know. Dialogue is merely a means for the characters to get, resist, accept (and so on) what they want. The action must come first, otherwise we will simply have verbiage, and no matter how witty or well written, the audience will lose interest.

Before commencing your third draft it is worth just going right back to the beginning of your journey. Look again at the genesis of your idea. Remind yourself what spurred you to write the play in the first place. Return to the well that was the original source of your water. This will freshen up your thinking. It is very easy in the process of writing a play – with all the conflicting interests of structure, plot, character and staging – to lose sight of what it was that inspired you in the first place and fuelled this journey that you have set yourself on.

What next?

So you've finished your third draft. Once again, put some distance between the play and yourself. Go away and do something else. When you return to your work you will want to ask yourself if your characters are now as familiar to you as people you have known all your life. Try the exercise from the earlier checklist where you try abstracting the character from the drama they are in and see if you honestly know how they would react. How do they enter a room? How do they address their peers? How do they talk to people lower down the social order than them? How do they order a pint in your local?

If you are happy with your play you may decide to risk a rehearsed reading in front of an audience. Be very careful of this, though, as the last thing you want to do is to submit yourself to some sort of vox pop where, in the bar afterwards, you have eighty of your friends all telling you what they think you should do to your play. The purpose of this reading should be for you to witness the play in front of an audience, and try and hear it through their ears, view it through their eyes. People will, of course, comment and when they do you will have to filter their opinions. Ignore those who say things like 'Is all that swearing really necessary?', but if twenty people all feel the plot is hard to follow then it may be that they are worth listening to!

The notion of three drafts of your play cannot be adhered to in every instance. Sometimes your work will require many more drafts (though I think it's unlikely you could write a play with fewer). But beware of too much rewriting. There's a fine line between perfecting your work and destroying it through endless tinkering. Because of the unwillingness of theatres in the United States to take a punt on new writing, many new American plays are endlessly workshopped and rewritten in arid university environments, and as a result arrive lifeless on the artistic director's desk. The initial passion that drove the play on – however dogmatic, however oversimplistic or however vengeful – has been destroyed and what you are left with is a very dry exercise. All the boxes are ticked but the play fails to catch fire. I think this is why many successful plays are thought about long and hard, but written very quickly.

The great thing about a play is that it doesn't require an awful lot of words. It is not a novel using hundreds of thousands of words which will be pored over by the reader. Plays can be written and rewritten very quickly, in intense bursts of creativity when the belief is there, when the passion is there, and when the blood is coursing through the veins, propelling you on, so you can get to the end . . .

PART THREE

Getting It On

Sending out your play

When?

This is one of the hardest decisions you will have to make. Send your play out too early and you may kill the baby at birth. Send it too late, after too many drafts, and you may find you have sucked the lifeblood out of it. Somebody else may come along and deliver a script with a similar idea and you may be pipped at the post. There are no prizes for coming second: the minute you spot a bandwagon, it is already too late to jump on.

When I give my script to somebody I trust, I find it useful to sit in the room with him or her. When I look over someone's shoulder as they read my play, a weird thing happens. Watching my private world becoming a public act for the first time forces me to look at my work in a different way. It enables me to see the play through the eyes of the reader, foreshadowing its future life in the eyes and minds of a whole audience. The big question: Is your play something of which you are proud? If so, go to the Post Office and buy some stamps.

Fear of rejection is one of the major reasons why writers don't buy the stamps and send their plays out. They avoid judgement being passed. The important thing to emphasise is that no play is perfect. Indeed, many directors, literary managers and actors will relish a script which has tons of life and energy, terrific scenes, a strong central idea – but which still leaves some room for improvement. Never underestimate the fact that human beings, and particularly directors and dramaturges, like to stick their oars in. All of us like to think we have contributed to whatever task we are involved in, and (good) actors and a director will, on the whole, have a positive effect on your work. But you must also fight to hold on to the play you want.

How?

Ideally your script should be typewritten, double-spaced, on A4 paper. Make sure it is printed in a clear font and that the pages are numbered. You may include a covering letter, but I would advise you to keep it brief and to the point. At this stage people are interested in your play, not your educational history or family background. The only exceptions I would make would be if you were submitting a play set in, for instance, a slaughterhouse or a bakery after having spent a period of time working there. In this case it might be worth saying, 'Please find enclosed my play *Doughnut*, which I wrote after a fun-packed year working in a Belfast bread factory.'

Try to avoid 'bigging yourself up' in the covering letter: it is the play that should remain the focus. It is important that you also include a stamped addressed envelope if you wish to have your play returned to you – otherwise your script will be 're-cycled' in the bin. If you are writing from outside the UK, enclose International Postal Coupons. Most theatres do not accept scripts by e-mail.

Where?

In the UK there is a sort of 'new-writing establishment', and correspondingly a new-writing ecology which is gratifyingly strong compared to that found in other countries in Europe and the United States. (See Appendix 2 for a list of theatres and companies who regularly produce new plays.)

I wouldn't recommend sending out your play to every theatre you can think of, in a scattergun fashion. It smacks of desperation. You should choose the theatres and artistic directors you most respect and whose work you know and like. It is no good sending your play to an artistic director whose work you hate. Even if he or she chooses to produce your play, you are going to find it a disappointment. How dispiriting is it going to be to work for a year or more on a play, only to see it mauled and mutilated by some director you detest? Someone once said you should choose your theatres like you choose your church, and this is absolutely true. All theatres are not the same; all taste is very specific and subjective. Do your research.

The new-writing circle is quite small, the literary managers all know each other and talk to each other, and their readers often read for more than one theatre. When I was a literary manager, I had four or five thousand scripts pass across my desk over a four-year period, and it became very hard not to groan, 'Oh, it's that play by John Smith again' when something turned up for the umpteenth time. Treat your work with respect: it is your child; send it out somewhere you passionately think it belongs.

Think imaginatively. You could always send it to a leading actor. If you had, say, Michael Gambon on board, I would find it very surprising if you could not find a commercial producer or a subsidised theatre (or both) to produce your work. Sometimes the new writing that is produced is not just about the best plays. Even in the subsidised sector, tickets still have to be sold. Shows can make a loss but no one can run a theatre that, however well-reviewed, is consistently empty. No cast wishes to be put through the agony of playing to rows of empty seats. So it is not at all shameful to think commercially.

You might send your play to an established freelance director whom you admire or have a relationship with, and let him or her present it to those new-writing theatres. This would give you an immediate leg-up. However, be wary of 'signing it over' to any director for an indefinite period. This would give them exclusive rights to direct the play and you might find yourself in the situation where a theatre wants to produce your play but with a different director, and your path is blocked. Agree to let the freelance director present it to theatres but only for a certain amount of time and if they don't succeed, their 'exclusivity option' ends. Even if the director or actor of your choice rejects it, they may well give you feedback or pass it on to a protégé who can make a production happen. The theatre world is quite small and people do pass on projects to other people.

Commercial managements

These can be an option if you genuinely think your play is commercial. Remember the priorities of commercial producers are entirely different from those of the subsidised sector. To mount a play in the West End costs from £150,000 to £500,000, and the list of straight plays which have recouped their outlay over the last five years is small and seems to get smaller each year.

If a commercial management sees potential in your script, they are more likely to 'get into bed' with a subsidised theatre and co-produce your play in what is a more protected and less financially demanding environment to begin with. It has been known that plays which have been turned down by subsidised theatres are then produced in those very same theatres because a commercial management has come on board. It may be the end of the subsidised theatre's financial year and they simply need a show to fill the slot. Bear in mind that there is no such thing as a 'free lunch' and in return for investing £25,000 or £50,000 in your production, the commercial producer is likely to want some say in how the play develops, in the choice of actors, directors and designers and in the way your show is marketed.

The days of opening a brand new play cold in the West End are largely gone. The only conceivable way this is likely to happen is for you to get a big star on board with huge box-office appeal – or you get a mad millionaire who has made a fortune in flat-pack kitchen units to invest in your production.

Whatever you think of the commercial theatre, if you are to make your fortune as a playwright, you will have to get involved with it. There are fortunes to be made: the most commercially successful entertainment of the twentieth century was not a Hollywood blockbuster but a British stage musical, *The Phantom of the Opera*. There is an old theatre truism that most writers don't make a living, but a few make a killing. In Yasmina Reza's case, she made a fortune largely based on just one play (*Art*)!

The Edinburgh Festival Fringe

An alternative and much more accessible route to getting your play on the stage is the Edinburgh Festival Fringe, which continues to be a wonderfully erratic and infuriating lottery. The number of shows staged every year continues to grow, but you can count the good work on the fingers of one hand. What is wonderful about Edinburgh is that anyone and everyone can put on a show there; entry into the Fringe is not based on any artistic criteria at all. But a word of warning: it is not cheap. You are talking a bare minimum of £5,000 to produce a play in Edinburgh to any sort of standard, and that figure wouldn't include an expensive set or paying your cast much, if at all. Just paying for your publicity and your entry into the official Fringe brochure, along with your accommodation, travel and living expenses, can easily set you back £3 – 4,000 and the odds on you recouping that are close to zero.

The best way to approach Edinburgh is to expect to lose all your money. That way, you can get on and enjoy the experience and exploit it to its fullest extent. Edinburgh is a great place to launch something, and given that it happens in August, the annual 'silly season' in the national press, it is possible to generate lots of coverage if your show has a 'sexy' or eccentric angle. If your play is a perfectly respectable, solid but old-fashioned piece of work, it may easily get overlooked by audiences and critics alike. On the other hand, it is possible to get a disproportionate amount of praise for a show in Edinburgh because, by and large, the standard is pretty uneven so anything even half decent stands a chance of a favourable notice from jaded critics.

Quite often the Fringe becomes akin to a giant party at which no one can quite find where the alcohol is, so all the critics and audiences spend their time moving from room to room, theatre to theatre, desperate to try and find some life and excitement. The minute they find anything with remotely any life in it, there is a tendency to overpraise. This applies to producers too, who get carried along on the Edinburgh euphoria, believing that 'hit' shows can be transferred to London or wherever. Occasionally it does happen. *Jerry*

Springer – The Opera had a try-out run in Edinburgh (after a small-scale experimental production at Battersea Arts Centre) and as a result was taken up by the National Theatre and subsequently transferred to the West End.

Literary agencies

At this stage you really don't have to have an agent to represent you, and if your play is taken up for a full production at a major theatre you will pretty soon acquire one anyway. Agents do carry weight and if your script arrives at a theatre with the stamp of one of the main London literary agencies on it, then it will almost certainly be read more quickly and by someone more senior. That said, waiting for a response from an agent will delay getting the script to the people who can make all the difference to your career: the producing theatres.

I'd be inclined to send the play to an agent at the same time as you send it to theatres. But do your research first. Visit the agents' websites and look at the people they already represent. Do they have writers whose work you like? Is any particular agent's taste likely to chime with yours? (See Appendix 4 for some of the major literary agencies.)

You're on!

If you are lucky enough to receive the letter that says a theatre wants to produce your play, what should you do? Firstly, try to extract definite dates from them and, more importantly, a contract. It's not that people deliberately set out to mislead, but circumstances change, money may get tight, staff may change, another play may come along. If they want to marry you, push for a date!

After that, I suggest you celebrate. Get very drunk and telephone all your friends to show off and tell your mother that she was wrong all along. You could also think about going out and buying a new car or putting down the deposit on a flat in Notting Hill – actually, forget those last two suggestions.

If your play has been accepted and will be produced by a theatre, you should be realistic about the money involved. It is pretty small. You will probably earn a few thousand pounds, maybe £5000, but don't forget that this amount may effectively have taken you a year of writing to earn. If the play goes on to future productions you will earn some more money. If it is published you will earn a small advance, but again we are not talking a lot of money, maybe £500–1000. If there is real money to be made, it will come from future productions, from a commercial transfer, from foreign translations and productions, and amateur performing rights. However, this is a terribly important stage in your career because you have got your feet on the first rung of the ladder. You will be a professionally produced playwright in a theatre. You will become part of that theatre's history, your name will appear on the radar, and you will become part of the theatrical ecosystem.

Getting an agent

If you haven't got one already, now is the best time to go for meetings with agents. You have a play coming up, people will want to read it and meet you. It is not love that engenders jealousy but jealousy that engenders love; the biggest fear for an agent is that you may become the 'next big thing' and will be snatched from under their nose by a rival. This will be their spur to meeting you and is most likely a reversal of the power situations you have found yourself in so far in your career. Some of these agents will want to meet you simply *because* you have a play coming up, and it really is important that, however grateful you are, you do not accept the first offer that's made. As with much else in this industry, the most important thing is to find an agent you actually like – one you think you can get on with – because the relationship you form together is terribly important. It's not dissimilar to a marriage, and it may be a marriage that lasts throughout your entire career.

At the same time, it's no good going with an agent you like but who actually has no clout. You want an agent who has clout and is hungry to push new talent. Take a look at who the agent already represents, and what sort of writers they are. Ask them where he or she thinks you should be going as a writer, and how they see your career panning out. The agents who can magically deliver lots of great work immediately are few and far between. Think very carefully before signing on the dotted line with anyone. In terms of fees, you will probably be giving up at least ten per cent of your earnings and you may have to give up fifteen per cent of your foreign earnings. You will also be charged VAT on payments which, if you are not VAT registered, will cost you. On the plus side, it will make accounting easier for you at the end of the year as most reputable agencies will send you a full statement of account more or less ready for the tax man.

You don't have to have an agent before your first production takes place. Most of the contracts issued by the majority of new-writing theatres are based on the standard Independent Theatre Council (ITC) contract or variations of it. It's unlikely, therefore, particularly in a subsidised theatre, that an agent will be able to get you more money. That said, it is extremely useful to have someone to look over the legal aspects of the document and, more importantly, someone in whom you can confide if you are not happy with how things are going during pre-production of your play. The agent can do your 'dirty work', complaining to the management, arguing your case, without you having to do it directly, potentially jeopardising your relationship with the people you are working with closely. And then, if your agent oversteps the mark with the management and asks too much (even if it's you who demanded it), you can blame the agent. However, you have to be realistic about the sort of demands your agent can make on your behalf. Agents will be reluctant to threaten their relationship with a particular theatre (unless they think you have a cast-iron case) since they have other clients who may want to work there in the future.

Getting a publisher

Now you are about to be a produced playwright, you have a much better chance of securing a publisher. Some theatres will have publishers they often work with and they will produce a combined playscript/programme, which goes on sale at a discounted price during the run of the play before reverting to its full price in bookshops after the run. Other theatres may leave you to your own devices, and allow you and your agent to approach publishers. Some theatres will not even bother if the play is published and available to sell or not.

You need to be realistic about the amount of money you can expect to receive by way of an advance from a publisher. You will be lucky to receive more than a thousand pounds and may have to settle for less, and it will be a long time (if ever) before you earn back that advance and start to accrue actual royalties. It is still highly desirable to be a published author as it greatly increases the chance of other people picking up your play and staging it, in both professional and amateur productions. The latter can be a very lucrative source of income (just ask Alan Ayckbourn, Amanda Whittington or John Godber). Publication also means that if you wanted to supplement your playwriting income by teaching in the creative-writing department of a university, you are a more attractive proposition to the academic community as your publications now count as 'research' and enable the institution to secure public funding towards your wages.

You should be aware that is highly unlikely that the published text (at least in its first edition) will be completely accurate. The book will almost certainly have to go to press before the end of the rehearsal process when changes are still being made to the script, though it is hoped these changes will be small and relatively insignificant. This is simply a fact of life and you just have to hope that your play sells enough copies to make it to a second edition when you can correct the inaccuracies and omissions. The relationship you have with your publisher is akin to the one you form with your agent and may last throughout your career, so choose wisely. (See Appendix 5 for a list of the UK's major play publishers.)

Production team

Choosing a director

The theatre may want you to do more work on your play, but this is probably more likely to happen once a director comes on board. No matter how much the literary manager or artistic director of the theatre likes your play, any director coming to it will have his or her own views. Most new-writing theatres will involve you in the choice of who should direct your work, and it's terribly important that you are happy with the decision. Don't just go out and read past reviews of a prospective director's work: make it your business to have seen it. The writer-director relationship is crucial and will play a large part in determining whether your play is a success or not. Working with a living playwright on a new play is a very different skill from reviving a classic text and you want the director to be someone who understands the process.

When meeting prospective directors, do not be afraid to question them about your play. Try and determine why they want to do it. Is it just a job for them or a career 'leg-up'? Or do they have a genuine passion for your work? If so, is that a passion to try and direct the play you have written or to impose their own mark? Good directing is, of course, a combination of both, but be wary of the director who wants to 'stage it on skates' just for the sake of it! In Britain, the theatre culture is very supportive of its writers, with the written text generally treated with respect and remaining central to the finished production. In Europe, the onus often lies more with the director, and the writer must be careful not to lose control over what they have written. This 'director's theatre' – daring interpretations and bold visions, not necessarily best serving the text – is gradually becoming more common in Britain, so be prepared for a battle of ideas if you come across a director of the European school.

When you first meet a prospective director, don't just sit in a stuffy office; go out for a drink or dinner, go and see a show or a film together – this can be very revealing. See whether you share the same sort of taste, see whether you laugh about the same sort of things. Does this director understand your sense of humour? Do they understand the world that your play is set in? They don't have to have been to Bradford to direct a play set there, but any director worth their salt will plan a trip there prior to rehearsals. They need to get a feel for the world they are attempting to direct a play about. If the director does have ideas for changes to your play, try and ascertain what they are beforehand, to see if they make sense to you. A good director will enhance your play, and you will want to make sure that the script you begin rehearsals with is better than the script you talked about at your first meeting. A bad director will have you running around in circles. Listen to them. Are they waffling? Do they make numerous points about this, that and the other? Do they have clarity? Look for a director who keeps things simple. Someone who has the ability to boil very complex things down to clear instructions that are achievable when you are rewriting. Be wary of those who over-intellectualise the process. In the end, this is all about putting on a show, not staging a debate.

*

When you are starting out, do not consider directing your own work. It is hard enough as the writer to get the play right, but to do so whilst also wearing the hat of the director is extremely difficult. You will find yourself not knowing whether the problems in the rehearsal room lie with the play, the direction or the acting. Boundaries will become blurred, and, more crucially, your own insecurities about the work (which are inevitable if you are less experienced) will be transmitted to the actors. Very soon your entire edifice will become fragile.

There are exceptions of course (Harold Pinter, Alan Ayckbourn, Conor McPherson and Nina Raine have all proved fine interpreters of their own work), but many is the time I have seen writers destroy their own play because they directed it themselves. Your proximity to the material, your inability to see it from a different perspective and your lack of objectivity will often prove crippling. I have sometimes directed the second or third production of some of my plays. Having seen the play work in the hands of a skilled director, it is much easier to direct these productions yourself. But when you are starting out, get yourself a good director who is not you.

Choosing a designer

Many directors have designers with whom they have worked before. You should meet them too. Talk to them about their ideas, about how they plan to realise the world you have created. Make sure the designer shares your vision. As with the director, be wary of the designer who simply wants to make their mark on your play. The last thing you want is the audience to go out 'humming the set'.

A great design can, of course, make a good production better. Stephen Daldry revived J.B. Priestley's old repertory warhorse *An Inspector Calls* with a set by Ian MacNeil which no one who saw the production will ever forget. Not only did MacNeil put the Birling family home on stilts but he located it in a Beckettian wasteland. When the family's internal world collapsed, the set went with it, literally exploding to pieces. The designer successfully married the director's express-ionistic vision of the play with a spectacular design, which allowed the audience to see a familiar play in a fresh way. As a result the production became more political, more urgent – and an enormous international success. But for every good design that makes a play better, there's a bad one that can upstage it.

Choosing the actors

Even if you feel you do not know the names of many actors, you should also be involved in the process of casting, and a good director will want you to be. When I was working at The Bush Theatre, the Artistic Director at the time, Mike Bradwell, would ask playwrights to name any person, living or dead, in any field, who they thought would be perfect for the characters they had written. Another exercise that can be useful is 'fantasy casting', where you name your absolute dream cast, even if there is no hope of actually getting Robert De Niro to appear at a fringe theatre in Edinburgh. These exercises are all about getting you to think about how you see your characters, and giving the director as much insight as possible into your thinking, rather than feeling you must suggest a list of actors' names or, worse, start thinking, 'I'd like him off the telly cos he's famous.'

Despite what I've just said about Robert De Niro, when you do approach casting, it's always worth aiming for your 'A' list. You never know what might happen; even very fine, very famous, totally appropriate actors have gaps in their schedule, or may just be taken with the idea of appearing in your play. It may be that your script has personal resonances for them. Think big – at least to start with.

Being involved in casting can also be useful for the final honing of your play. Hearing fifteen or twenty actors reading the same part will often give you a very clear idea of the character: when they are speaking in their 'true voice' and when they are not. You may discover a part is underwritten or that actors are not interested in playing some tiny part you have created. If you have difficulty getting actors to come to a meeting or to read for a certain part, ask yourself, 'Is that part worth getting out of bed for?' Actors in smaller theatres may be facing a three- to four-week rehearsal period and a six-week run playing to fifty to a hundred people a night, all on Equity minimum wages of a few hundred pounds. Place yourself in their shoes, and look on the job of the writer as giving the actor something to work with. Have you given them enough to do? Does the part look fun? I know the old adage, 'There is no such thing as a small part, only small actors.' But there is also such a thing as a lack of interest in small parts. There can also be brilliant small parts; an actor might have only one scene, but it's possible that it is so well written that they can steal the entire show.

You may also get feedback from actors about the play that will help you in the future. Use the time when you are listening to actors read your work to get some three-dimensional sense of the play you have written. It can be a fascinating process. An actor may improvise something that you can 'steal'. An actor may capture the voice of your character so well at a given point that you feel you can rewrite other sections in that style, with much greater clarity.

When you are seeing actors, try not to predetermine what you want or what they should look like. You may have a fixed image in your mind of how your characters should appear, but if somebody comes into the rehearsal room who is a foot smaller and three stone heavier than you envisaged, but they read the part brilliantly, ask yourself if it could work. Thinking outside the box and having an open mind in this situation is important. It's that difficult balancing act of knowing your mind, but being open to change if a better idea comes along. It is also important to cast a group of actors who you think can work well together, who have the flexibility and intelli-gence to help develop the play. From here on in, this is a team endeavour. The spirit of your company will communicate itself on stage. If the actors are enjoying themselves, the audience will too.

Above all else, pay attention to the casting process as there's a lot of truth in the belief that the success of a production is seventy-five per cent in the casting. The decisions the director takes before rehearsals begin often have as much bearing on the success of the production as the decisions taken during them. By that time, if the production is miscast, it is simply too late, and you will merely be 'rearranging the deckchairs on the *Titanic*'.

Publicity

In the frantic fight for an audience it's inevitable that you will have some role to play in the publicity and marketing of the production, if only to approve the publicity image, the leaflet copy and programme material. The press and marketing department of a theatre may also call on you to be available to be interviewed in the press, on radio or – very rarely – on television, especially if there's a reason why you're potentially 'newsworthy' (e.g. it's a regional theatre and you're a local writer). Be open and helpful to all ideas that are put your way and never dismiss them as a distraction. You've spent many months labouring over your play. Now you want people to see it!

Titles

This may seem a trivial point – and by this stage it's probably been decided on for months – but titles can make or break a play. To that end, think very carefully about the title you have at present. Is it the one you really want and, more importantly, is it one that an impartial theatregoer flicking through listings would choose to go and see? I've often seen writers stubbornly stick to a boring title because they think it most truthfully represents their work of art, and then wonder why the box-office advance is small. You really won't be pleased that you held on to your pretentious title if the show doesn't sell.

Beware of titles that sound pretentious or intellectual because even though there are some *Time Out* readers dashing round London from one major 'cultural event' to the next, these are not in the majority. The title needs to capture the play, to give a flavour of it without giving the game away. It needs to hint at the genre of the play without being too 'on the nose'. It should contain an implicit question that makes an audience want to see it, to make them feel excited, perhaps even make them smile – but above all it should make them want to book their tickets!

If the director or producer or management of the theatre questions the title, then write a long list of all the possible titles and road-test them on friends and colleagues. I am completely against road-testing plays and asking what sample audiences think of them, but when it comes to titles, images and leaflets, it's very different. This is the point at which you are actively engaging with the audience by trying to entice them into coming to see your play. Mark Ravenhill's *Shopping and Fucking* is one of the best contemporary titles: audacious, cheeky, provocative and shocking, just like the play.

Leaflet copy

Like the title, the leaflet will play a large part in determining what your advance bookings are like; it's much easier to have a hit from strong advance sales than a 'cold start'. Some playwrights are very good at writing promotional copy, and some are absolutely dreadful. Likewise, some marketing departments are good copywriters and some are appalling! I'd suggest you have a go at writing some copy yourself and also let the theatre's team have a go. I've often found that the best copy lies somewhere in between. The purpose of the copy is not to spell out your thesis or to tell the audience what the play is about; it is to get them to come and see it. Make it sound exciting, lively and worth getting out of the house for. Read lots of other leaflets and analyse why the ones you like work so well.

Programme notes

Be wary of writing lengthy programme notes explaining what your play is about. I can list numerous occasions when the critical response to a writer's play has been completely hijacked by their programme notes. The critics end up reviewing the notes and comparing it to your play: 'Mr Smith claims that his play is about globalisation and the homogenisation of culture. Well frankly, it's about three men in a shack.' Given half the chance, they will use your pronouncements as a stick with which to beat you. Consequently, I would avoid programme notes at all costs.

In your biography it is better to put that this is your 'first play' than to list lots of obscure fringe productions, because critics like to think they have discovered a new talent delivered from the gods. Of course writers rarely come from nowhere. Ravenhill's *Shopping and Fucking* was supposed to have emerged from the ether as a miraculous debut, successful overnight. But the play was actually given a try-out at the Finborough Theatre in London way before theatre company Out of Joint picked it up and took it to the Royal Court. And who knows much about Mark Ravenhill's early student bingo play which was written before that? If you happen to have a background in television then I would keep quiet about it. I'm afraid the theatre critics are very snobbish. Time and again I have seen reviews saying something like, 'Ms Smith has written for soap opera and it shows.' Do not give your 'enemies' ammunition: they have enough firepower of their own!

Interviews

It may also be at this stage you will be starting to give interviews, and these will set the tone for the way in which your play is perceived. The odds are that if it is a new play and it's your first play, there won't be that many interviews; maybe a few with local newpapers, radio stations and theatre websites. It's very important to get a sense of who will be reading or listening to what you're saying. For example, there's little point doing a local radio-station interview and going into the intricacies of postmodernism. Keep it simple: make the play sound fun and entertaining and drop names of actors if anyone might have heard of them. If your play bears any similarities to a more famous film or book, then mention that too ('It's *Doctor Zhivago* for the iPod generation.'). Remember you are trying to get bums on seats!

I try and make interviews fun. This can be hard if they are telephone conversations with someone you have never met before. In this instance I would try and ensure that you do the interview at a time of your choosing, when you are relaxed. It may seem ridiculous, but finding a comfortable seat and having a glass of something in your hand (even a non-alcoholic one) can make all the difference. Politely refuse to do a telephone interview if you are in the middle of rehearsals when you feel distracted and insecure, as this will be communicated to the interviewer and may seep into the interview when it's written up or broadcast.

To quote Quentin Crisp, when being interviewed 'say what you have come to say, no matter what.' If you have a story you want to tell about your mother and the interviewer asks about your father, you reply: 'My father is worn out coping with my mother *who* . . . ' Have two or three things you think are worth saying about the play and make sure you say them. Most interviewers will be grateful that you have given them a couple of juicy quotes or soundbites. I like to go into press interviews relaxed and strike up a rapport with the person interviewing me before we get onto the subject of the play. If people like you, they are much more likely to write useful copy than if you appear difficult or aloof.

Don't become a poodle, all smarmy and obsequious; stick to your guns if you disagree with your interviewer. Don't posture; be yourself. People are never at their best when they are being 'at their best'. Try and relax. If you have a couple of funny stories from rehearsals then tell them. Try not to make the interview monotonous. Be wary of making grandiloquent claims for your play; don't exaggerate the 'importance' of your work even before it has been produced. Be the writer you are, in the situation you are in. It's your first play; you are very excited about it. You hope it is going to go well; it's based on your family background, where you came from . . . Things that make you come across as a human being can make the readers or listeners feel that the play might be worth seeing because it is clearly written by another human being.

Rehearsals

A four-week rehearsal period is what you should hope for, although you may get even less (sometimes just a week for a pantomime!). How much exploration and how much rewriting can be done over such a short time? That will depend on the director and the actors you are working with. During the first week of rehearsal many new-writing theatres will pay you an attendance fee to be there, and you should certainly be present when you can. You will be able to rewrite, but you must do this judiciously and in co-operation with the director. It is no good going away every night and coming back the next day with a new scene, giving it to the actors and expecting it all to work. The actors will start to lose faith and fall back into ingrained habits rather than exploring the new terrain that is your play. In attempting to make your play better, you will end up destroying it.

First day

The first day of rehearsals is the most exciting and terrifying moment of the process so far. The cast, the director, the designer, the backstage staff, the lighting and sound designers, all the administrative staff from the theatre, and maybe even the front-of-house staff will all come together to hear the play read aloud. It puts an incredible pressure on the actors to deliver a performance there and then, but this is the last thing you want them to do, since they will start to make decisions which get set in stone before the rehearsal process has actually begun.

This read-through can be a traumatic experience too because the play will not fully 'work'. In fact, it may seem to fail so badly that you want to disown it. Keep a sense of perspective. The backstage technical team have been working late on the current show and will probably yawn, the staff from the development office may be worrying about where all the funding will come from, and the front-of-house staff just wish they were you. You may find, as you look around the room, a sea of blank faces. Block these out and listen to the play for yourself. This is a ring of fire that has to be passed through.

You may find that the actors 'mug' like crazy and play every moment for laughs; all kinds of weird things may happen which will leave you thinking: 'What have I written? Why has the theatre programmed this play?' This is why the relationship you have with an experienced director is important: you may need someone to hold your hand at this stage and you may require a strong drink afterwards. Never forget the fable of the tortoise and the hare: the plays with the best response at the read-through stage don't always end up becoming the most successful productions when finally on stage.

First week

In the first week of rehearsals it is vital that you are there. But you need to establish a way of giving feedback, via the director, which does not upset the actors. The great difficulty for actors in a new play, when the writer is present in the rehearsal room, is that they think you know all the answers. They will be looking to you for a reaction. If you suddenly pipe up, your words will carry more weight than the director's because the actors view you as the unique authority. You may know quite a lot but you will also have some completely ridiculous ideas about your own play. Often I have found I have a very strong idea of what the subtext of a given scene is, but I'm unable to see the 'surface action' the actors need to play in order to make the scene credible.

You must establish a working method with the director which involves watching what is happening in rehearsal without appearing to judge. If you are frowning, grimacing or laughing out loud, the actors will take note of this, and it will affect what they are doing. If you laugh on day one and day two, and then don't laugh on day three, they will be convinced they are getting something wrong. So both praise and criticism have to be rationed.

A significant temptation for the writer in rehearsal is to try and get the actors to their destination of a finished performance on day one. This is absolutely disastrous and can destabilise the cast, completely blocking a thorough exploration of character and text. If it were possible to stage your play as perfectly as you would like on the first day, then rehearsals would be scrapped. You have embarked on a journey, so do not expect results immediately. In fact, be fearful of productions that seem to achieve results too early since, by the time they open, they might simply have passed their sell-by date or gone off the boil. The best directors bring the pan to the boil at exactly the right time.

Keep some sense of perspective and objectivity in the rehearsal room. This may mean taking yourself away from it. Try not to watch the rehearsal with your head buried in your text, checking that the actor is saying every word – this is very off-putting. Actors want to feel you are enjoying what they are doing, not looking away from it. Good acting, good writing and good directing can only occur when things are relaxed; the more tension there is in the rehearsal room, the worse the situation will get. You only have to see what happens to a cast on press night to see what tension can do. Try and keep the tension away. You, as a writer, appearing relaxed will get the best from your cast; appearing tense will sow seeds of doubt. Of course you *will* be tense, but share that with the director at lunch, or in the bar afterwards. Do not share it with the actors.

After the first week

At the end of the first or second week the director ought to be thinking about sending the writer out shopping. There comes a point when your familiarity with the script will lead you to be of little use in the rehearsal room. It is important that you retain some sense of an 'audience's eye' over the show. You must maintain the integrity and vision of your work but also now, with it on its feet, and the actors beginning to act with props on a designed set, you should start to see it like the audience sees it. You are approaching a point after which any alterations you can make to the text will be minimal.

Go away from the rehearsals for a couple of days. It can be fun trying to distract yourself by going out with the assistant stage manager to buy props, or with the designer to hunt for costume fabric. Do things that maintain your sense of perspective, because by this stage the production will have induced tunnel vision in you. It is a wonderful thing when you have that level of focus and intensity in the work, but it is also very dangerous if objectivity is lost. Bill Shankly, the former manager of Liverpool Football Club, famously said that 'Football isn't a matter of life and death; it's more important than that.' This is how your first professionally produced play will feel to you: it will mean more to you than anything else you have done creatively in your life. It will feel like the ultimate test and challenge of your talent and nerve. You will feel the spotlight of the world is trained upon you. In reality, yours is just one of any number of productions that are about to open in any number of cities in any number of countries in the world. And more to the point, normal life is going on around you, so trying to retain some sense of that is terribly important. There is nothing worse – or more self-centred – than a rehearsal room which becomes infected with a destructive intensity, and in which people lose their sense of perspective and proportion.

Final rehearsals

The first few days of rehearsals and you are absolutely euphoric. Everything seems to be going swimmingly; the words are fresh; you think your play is a total smash. You then hit the point where you have heard the words too many times – so have the actors – and your play starts to lose its shine. What was once funny is no longer even mildly amusing, what induced tears on day one seems now to be risibly overblown.

From the director to the box-office staff, everyone's nerves will be frayed. Everyone has a stake in your production. Your work is the absolute centre of everything that is happening in that theatre at that time. It is everything you have worked for and everything you have ever dreamed about, and it is absolutely terrifying. Hold your nerve. Do not make major changes to your script. This is the time where the director and actors have to make the best of what they have got and everyone has to compromise to some extent, including you.

You then have the even more hair-raising moment when the actors have to put down their scripts, and invariably the whole thing falls apart. Suddenly, what a week and a half ago looked like being a sure-fire hit now looks like the turkey of the century. You hope and pray that the actors are going to get it right and the play will soar.

In the final week the lighting, sound and any special effects will be introduced, and the technical rehearsal will take place. Personally, I don't think the writer should be there for the tech. It's not about the acting or the writing; it is for the director and the technical team (lighting, sound, stage management) to work together in order to get the mechanics of the production ticking over: making sure the props work, that the fridge light comes on, that the switch on the wall does turn the fan on and that the phone rings and stops ringing at the right moment. It can be a frustrating time for the actors because up to this point everything has been about their acting, and then suddenly the director shifts his focus to technical matters. There is no point in you being there because you won't see your play at its best and there are already enough people having their say. The interesting thing, though, is that the actors sometimes relax as technical checks go on around them and the attention is off them. The conditions are right for them to produce performances so good that they are not seen again until the end of the run when the pressure is again removed.

The next instrument of torture designed to test your nerve is the dress rehearsal. In the professional theatre, where time will allow, there are normally at least two dress rehearsals. The first will probably be a ropey 'stagger-through' which stops and starts every time things go wrong. Sound cues might be in the wrong place; the scene changes in chaos; the actors forgetting their lines. If you are present at this rehearsal you must bite your tongue. Everyone will be doing their best (even if it doesn't seem so to you), so shouting and storming out helps no one.

Depending on which theatre you are working in, the second dress rehearsal may well be the last chance for the director and for you to see the show before the audience sees it. This is the time to get through the play at all costs, no matter what goes wrong. Actors who forget their lines should make them up; if the lights fall from the ceiling they are pushed off the stage discreetly and the show carries on. Everyone will be scared but the one thing that the director wants to see is the production from beginning to end. No matter how many times you sit through a dress rehearsal, you'll still always wonder if your play is fit to put in front of an audience.

Your role is to be very supportive – if you still have to make notes, do it discreetly. Sit at the back, otherwise you may end up putting off the actors and getting a worse performance, not a better one. If you have any feedback, give it to the director. Try to ignore the neurosis and fear that will be pulsing through your system. Some writers like to have friends at the final dress rehearsal or an open dress rehearsal (where friendly 'insiders' are invited along to give the actors something to play to), but this is a decision for the director and the actors. The cast will have reached the point where they are sick to the back teeth of playing the same old lines to the same old reaction from the same old faces, so a new audience will help to lift things. Be careful about the people you invite. You need people you can trust to keep their own counsel and be constructively critical and supportive, people of good taste whose opinions you trust.

Performances

First preview

You won't actually have that many previews in new-writing theatres; maybe a couple of days to a week. Previews in New York last so long that you feel like the play is over before it finally opens (indeed, some plays close in preview!). You can't expect a preview to be perfect, and stuff will go wrong. The crucial thing at this stage is that the director is able to encourage the actors to 'leap off the high-dive'. There comes a point where all the talking and preparation, the months of writing and rehearsals, and all the agonising have to be set aside and a gigantic leap has to be made. In some productions that leap is never made. The actors never jump off to play, enjoy, react in the present tense. They certainly won't or can't if they are frozen with fear and doubt. In order to serve your play, you also have to encourage them to have fun, to play, to enjoy. It is the equivalent of spending weeks, months or years walking around a beautiful swimming pool, then finally diving in and splashing around.

In front of an audience your play will take a completely different form. The performances will rise and fall, will acquire focus and precision, and you as a writer will begin to see whether your play works or not. Until this stage you can never, ever be sure. Every great writer has written flops, often after successive hits. Only a hack would be able to turn out consistent, moderate success. If you have taken risks, as you should have done, then this is a danger area. Embrace the fear. Be proud of the risks you have taken.

The next day the director will call the actors in for notes and feedback. This will last for the whole day or half a day depending on how it has gone. Things will be reworked; the odd line may be cut. In exceptional circumstances you may cut a whole scene, although I'd be extremely worried if you were cutting scenes this late in the process. But remember you cannot be writing new scenes. There is no time for the actors to learn them!

Second preview

From a technical perspective, the second preview should be more adept, but the acting during the first preview will have been elevated by a massive adrenaline rush caused by appearing in front of an audience for the first time. It's amazing how far adrenaline can carry a production. By the second preview it will have subsided slightly and the performance will not be quite as good as the first. So on the way to the theatre, prepare yourself for an element of disappointment. Invariably, I experience an arc of emotion which begins with absolute fear before the first preview, followed by total euphoria that it went brilliantly, followed by the realisation at the second preview that I was being carried away the night before: that there are good things but there are also imperfections, that there is still more work to be done and sadly some faults that it is too late to correct.

Press night (and reviews)

Unless the first few previews have been a cataclysmic disaster, and rehearsals need to carry on right up to the press night, a sensible director will try and preserve the energy and focus of the actors on this day. The worst thing that can be done is to call the cast for 10 a.m. and work them all day, so that they are in such a frazzled state they have nothing left to give in the performance. The actors are terrified; their careers are on the line every bit as much as yours. But fear is the impediment to creativity, so try to remain relaxed.

Press night is to be endured rather than enjoyed, I'm afraid. I have seldom been to a press night of mine and seen a performance which was as good as it could have been or as good as it would later become. It's hard for the play to fulfil its potential when it's so early in the run, and being played to such an unrepresentative audience. There will be a lot of largely middle-aged, middle-class, white men scribbling neurotically in their pads, complaining about their seats, and ready to race off during the curtain call to write up their reviews. The rest of the audience will have been invited by the theatre, so expect a supportive crowd who laugh in all the right places (though perhaps a little too much or too falsely), and cheer at the end until the applause is ringing in your ears.

You should be very careful where you place yourself – or where you ask the box-office staff to seat you. I would suggest you sit where the cast are least likely to see you. The last thing they want is to catch sight of you frowning, growling or gnawing your fingernails to the quick. Equally you don't want to sit amongst the critics. In the United States, the critics see the show on the previews before the first night, so that the reviews are printed around the time of the first night's after-show party. There are many legendary stories of parties coming to an abrupt end once a scathing *New York Times* review arrived. In the UK, there may be overnight reviews for the production, but you will be able to party on opening night, blissfully oblivious to what they will say. For now, you should celebrate the fact that you got to the end of writing your play, and then got it on.

*

Some people who work in theatre say that the reviews don't matter. If only that was true. You do have a choice as to whether you look at them and, if you do, how you interpret them. If, like me, you're unable to resist reading them then it's important to retain a sense of perspective. Often reviews will come out on different days. If you are lucky and your first review is great, you will then be able to stomach your second review being awful. But if your first review is awful then the pressure builds; and if your second and third reviews are in the same vein you will start to panic. Always remember that the critics are individuals with their own tastes and prejudices, and that they can get it spectacularly wrong!

It's also important to remember that the audience will not read the reviews with anything approaching the microscopic detail that you will! They might just look at the photo, the headline or the star rating. Their decision about whether or not to buy tickets to the production won't be made on the finer points of the review. Many times I have read reviews that weren't particularly good, but I've still wanted to see the show. Similarly, you can sometimes read a good review and still be put off from going because it doesn't sound like your cup of tea, or because the rave comes from a critic whose taste you don't trust.

A well-known former artistic director of the Royal Court Theatre used to telephone the press office to ask about the reviews. His first question would be 'Is it a colour picture?' The second question would be 'How big is it [the size of the article]?', and the third question, 'What does it say?' The impact of the review on the page is more important than what it actually says. I've frequently had highly informed friends congratulate me on fantastic reviews, when actually they've only seen preview articles and features, largely constructed from press releases issued by the theatre.

So keep your sense of perspective – that also applies if you find that your reviews are fantastic! If they say you are a genius, they are probably wrong; if they say you are a fool, they are probably wrong. And don't be dismayed if the reviews are deeply split. This can be a good thing in terms of box office – a middling three-star review will often provoke far fewer ticket sales than a conflicting range of no-star and five-star reviews.

But remember, above all else, that you didn't create your play for critics. You wrote it for the audience.

The run

With the agony of the opening out of the way, you can now return and see your play for fun, with real paying punters. However, I would recommend you have a few days off before doing this. It's important that you try and distance yourself from the creative process you have gone through and that you now start to see your work 'in action' through the eyes of the audience, as this will help you to learn most as a playwright. It's also vital that the writer and director let the actors take full possession of the show; it's hard for them to do that with you breathing down their necks night after night. A good play with a strong cast will grow and develop in performance and be shaped by the audience.

You might find when you return after a few days that the cast are becoming affected by the audiences' responses and are starting to play up to them. You may find things have crept into the production that you dislike. If this is so, it's important that you filter your notes through the director, otherwise discipline breaks down, the cast can start to hear conflicting voices before going on stage, and their performances will be ruined. Making theatre is a team game with morale and trust both absolutely central to success. Sometimes little lies have to be told and secrets kept for the greater good.

The end of the run

And so the fat lady sings. The last night's performance will probably be the best you have ever seen, partly for sentimental reasons, partly because the actors are now into their stride and free of any of the fear and inhibition that preoccupied the early stages of the run. The company will have a final post-show drink, vowing to keep in touch with each other for ever (a promise they may or may not keep). You too may have struck up relationships with the director and actors that you will wish to preserve. Writers who have had a good first experience with a director and actors will often go on to work with them again. Theatrical history is full of examples of long-lasting writer-director partnerships such as those of Caryl Churchill and

Max Stafford-Clark, David Hare and Richard Eyre, Simon Gray and Harold Pinter, and of playwrights whose work has been written especially for or been performed by the same actor.

Suddenly you will start thinking, 'Maybe this idea would be well directed by him' or 'That might be just right for that actress.' This is good: you are now entering the mindset of a professional writer. Try and maintain the good relationships you have struck up in this first production. Keep them alive. Having a professional network of directors, actors and designers whom you know and can work with will help you enormously and keep you believing in your own career.

This career on which you have embarked is a marathon not a sprint. Above all else at this stage, remember that no matter how the production has gone – whether it's sold all the seats or been a commercial disaster, well reviewed or not – you have achieved one of the hardest things: you have achieved a first professional production. You are a professionally produced playwright. You exist.

Your play's future

You may have been lucky: your play has been a hit and a commercial management has picked it up. This is a whole new game and at this stage you definitely need your hand held by an agent.

Once you have dealt with a commercial producer heading towards the West End, Broadway or on tour, the rules are different. These are people producing theatre in order to make money. They want to make a profit out of your play, and in order to do that, they have to invest large sums of money. A West End production can cost hundreds of thousand of pounds, all of which could be lost within a few weeks — and often is.

The things you didn't have to watch as keenly when you were working in the subsidised theatre sector – whether your name was on the poster, whether your programme credit is present and correct, etc. – you now have to scrutinise carefully. If the name of your show is going up outside a West End theatre, the last thing the producer will want to do is also pay for your name written out in bright lights. They will argue that your name won't sell any tickets, that no one has ever heard of you. However, unless your name does go up in lights, nobody *will* ever hear of you. Time and again I've turned up at openings of my shows to discover that my name has 'accidentally' been left off. It's an experience shared with fellow writer friends of mine – too often to be accidental?

Your future

During the run, 'TV vultures' will probably swoop in: script developers, script editors and producers 'seeking' new talent. They will invite you to meetings. Without wishing to sound too cynical, my advice would be to make them buy you lunch and be certain to have the pudding; at least that way you will get something out of it. If your play has been well reviewed there will be a stampede of such people, all desperate to get hold of what they perceive to be 'the next big thing'. They will promise you things that quite often they simply cannot deliver. Eighty per cent of the offers that come in the first few days of the opening of a new play will disappear into thin air. If you have an agent, discuss these offers to work out who you should meet and who you shouldn't; but don't rush into anything.

If your play is a success, you may well be approached by the management of the theatre where it has been produced, or by the management of some other new-writing theatre, and offered a commission for a second play. All of this is good news but be wary of signing up to too many things too quickly. Whilst the money will be very welcome, these projects will ultimately have to be delivered!

*

What if you are one of the thousands of playwrights whose work has not been produced? Should you give up? Only you can answer that. But if writing plays gives you pleasure, if the determination to improve fills you with excitement, then you will carry on. Many successful playwrights endured many knock-backs and rejections before finally seeing their work produced.

The career of Martin McDonagh, currently the most produced playwright in America, is proof that early rejection need not prevent later success. Many of his successful plays were written *before* his first hit, *The Beauty Queen of Leenane,* and were rejected by all the major new-writing theatres. Once *Beauty Queen* had been staged, productions of these other plays quickly followed to huge acclaim. So listen, learn and develop, but try to stick to your guns. The key is releasing your own voice, not mimicking others or writing to order.

*

If you *have* been lucky enough to have gone through the process described in this book, you will have seen your first play staged. You will have put your marker down on the map. You will be a player in the game.

This will bring with it pressures all of its own. How do you follow your success? How do you ensure your second play is not merely a reaction to the critical response of your first one? How do you avoid repeating yourself?

Thankfully these problems never go away and they are what make the life of a writer constantly fascinating. Your attempt to master language, content and form will cheerfully occupy the rest of your natural life. Like your characters, you have embarked on a journey full of highs and lows, but every day will present a delicious challenge. You will want to get better – and you will. You will want to tell the stories only you know.

AFTERWORD

In writing this book I have aimed to put into print some of my approaches to and beliefs about playwriting and what makes good theatre. I hope I have provided you with some signposts for your journey through the dense forest that is writing and producing a play. I hope, however, that this book does not overly intellectualise a process that has to be instinctive, and does not leave you feeling that playwriting is a science with certain rules which, if strictly followed, will lead to success. There are few rules and no guarantees of success.

Many of the finest theatre practitioners will tell you that their best productions were 'happy accidents'. Sure, their experience over many years contributed to the success, enabling them to eliminate fundamental mistakes, but in the end, the magical alchemy which creates great theatre is not conjured up by following a rulebook. So, as you go away to write your play, use and abuse this book as you see fit. Where it infuriates you, write abuse in the margin. Where it helps you, underline the passage(s) in thick red pen and send cheques to my agent.

However you choose to approach this strangest of art forms, remember that, above all else, storytelling is fundamental to our very existence. From the beginnings of time, humans have told one another tales. The stories we tell give shape and meaning to our lives. They allow us to journey into territory which scares us. They allow us to examine what life would be like, what it could be like and what it should be like.

But the mechanism for telling these stories has remained consistent since the days of the caveman. A small child knows instinctively that a story has a beginning, a middle and an end. An audience looks instinctively for that story. Remember, nobody was ever dull who told the truth. Only a lie is boring.

APPENDIXES

1. USEFUL RESOURCES

2. KEY THEATRES FOR NEW WRITING

London
Regions
Touring Theatre Companies

3. REGIONAL ORGANISATIONS
THAT SUPPORT PLAYWRIGHTS

4. LITERARY AGENCIES

5. PLAY PUBLISHERS

1. USEFUL RESOURCES

Print

These directories are available in most public libraries.

Contacts
A directory of entertainment industry contacts, published annually by The Spotlight. Includes listings of theatre producers, theatres and literary agencies.

Writers' & Artists' Yearbook
Annually updated directory of media contacts published by A&C Black. Includes listings of theatre producers and literary agencies, and a useful section on finance for writers!

Online

BBC Writersroom (www.bbc.co.uk/writersroom)
Information on events and competitions – for theatre as well as broadcast media.

Doollee (www.doollee.com)
A huge searchable database of plays written or produced in English since 1956. There's also a full listing of literary agencies, together with the playwrights they represent – very useful for doing your homework before you write that letter seeking representation.

Writernet (www.writernet.co.uk)
An online resource for playwrights, with useful listings of awards and competitions, funding bodies, writing courses, literary agencies and producing theatre companies. There is also a 'Writers Wanted' section listing employment opportunities (although this section is accessible only to subscribers) and a script-reading service (charges vary).

Writers' Guild of Great Britain (www.writersguild.org.uk)
The trade union representing writers in theatre and other
media.

2. KEY THEATRES FOR NEW WRITING

Most of the theatres below have literary departments who will read and assess your play. Sometimes they will send you a report on the play, even if it isn't accepted for production. This is an excellent way to get feedback, and to get your work known – it's often the writers who have been around a while who find themselves getting produced.

Before sending your script to any theatre, think carefully about what kind of play is generally produced there and whether yours is one that's likely to be seriously considered for production. And always check the theatre's website for guidance on submissions such as who to address it to, and what to include (most require a writer's CV and stamped addressed envelope for return of script).

London

The Bush Theatre
Shepherd's Bush Green, London W12 8QD
www.bushtheatre.co.uk

Finborough Theatre
118 Finborough Road, London SW10 9ED
www.finboroughtheatre.co.uk

Hampstead Theatre
Eton Avenue, London NW3 3EU
www.hampsteadtheatre.com

The National Theatre
South Bank, London SE1 9PX
www.nationaltheatre.org.uk

The Old Vic
The Cut, London SE1 8NB
www.oldvictheatre.com

Royal Court Theatre
Sloane Square, London SW1W 8AS
www.royalcourttheatre.com

Soho Theatre and Writers' Centre
21 Dean Street, London W1D 3NE
www.sohotheatre.com

Theatre 503
Latchmere Pub, 503 Battersea Park Road,
London SW11 3BW
www.theatre503.com

Theatre Royal, Stratford East
Gerry Raffles Square, London E15 1BN
www.stratfordeast.com

Tricycle Theatre
269 Kilburn High Road, London NW6 7JR
www.tricycle.co.uk

Regions

Birmingham Repertory Theatre
Broad Street, Birmingham B1 2EP
www.birmingham-rep.co.uk

Clwyd Theatr Cymru
Mold, Flintshire CH7 1YA
www.clwyd-theatr-cymru.co.uk

Contact
Oxford Road, Manchester M15 6JA
www.contact-theatre.org.uk

Derby Playhouse
Theatre Walk, Eagle Centre, Derby DE1 2NF
www.derbyplayhouse.co.uk

Hull Truck Theatre
Spring Street, Hull HU2 8RW (*relocating 2008*)
www.hulltruck.co.uk

Live Theatre
7-8 Trinity Chare, Quayside, Newcastle upon Tyne NE1 3DF
www.live.org.uk

Liverpool Everyman and Playhouse
13 Hope Street, Liverpool L1 9BH
www.everymanplayhouse.com

The New Wolsey Theatre
Civic Drive, Ipswich, Suffolk IP1 2AS
www.wolseytheatre.co.uk

Northern Stage
Barras Bridge, Newcastle upon Tyne NE1 7RH
www.northernstage.co.uk

Nottingham Playhouse
Wellington Circus, Nottingham NG1 5AF
www.nottinghamplayhouse.co.uk

Nuffield Theatre
University Road, Southampton SO17 1TR
www.nuffieldtheatre.co.uk

Oldham Coliseum Theatre
Fairbottom Street, Oldham OL1 3SW
www.coliseum.org.uk

Royal Exchange Theatre
St Ann's Square, Manchester M2 7DH
www.royalexchange.co.uk

Royal and Derngate Theatres
Guildhall Road, Northampton NN1 1DP
www.royalandderngate.co.uk

The Royal Shakespeare Company
Royal Shakespeare Theatre, Waterside,
Stratford-upon-Avon, Warwickshire CV37 6BB
www.rsc.org.uk

Stephen Joseph Theatre
Westborough, Scarborough YO11 1JW
www.sjt.uk.com

Sheffield Theatres
55 Norfolk Street, Sheffield S1 1DA
www.sheffieldtheatres.co.uk

Theatre Royal & Drum Theatre, Plymouth
Royal Parade, Plymouth PL1 2TR
www.theatreroyal.com

Traverse Theatre
10 Cambridge Street, Edinburgh EH1 2ED
www.traverse.co.uk

West Yorkshire Playhouse
Playhouse Square, Quarry Hill, Leeds LS2 7UP
www.wyplayhouse.com

Touring

Below is a selection of the major non-building-based theatre companies specialising in new writing.

7:84 Theatre Company
4 Summertown Road, Glasgow G51 2LY
www.784theatre.com

Eastern Angles
Sir John Mills Theatre, Gatacre Road, Ipswich,
Suffolk IP1 2LQ
www.easternangles.co.uk

HighTide Festival
Adam House, 7 Adam Street, The Strand,
London WC2N 6AA
www.hightidefestival.org

National Theatre of Scotland
Atlantic Chambers, 45 Hope Street, Glasgow G2 6AE
www.nationaltheatrescotland.com

New Perspectives Theatre Company
Park Lane Business Centre, Park Lane, Basford,
Nottingham NG6 0DW
www.newperspectives.co.uk

The New Works
13a Hope Street, Liverpool L1 9BQ
www.thenewworks.com

Out of Joint
7 Thane Works, Thane Villas, London N7 7PH
www.outofjoint.co.uk

Paines Plough
4th Floor, 43 Aldwych, London WC2A 4DN
www.painesplough.com

Pentabus
Bromfield, Ludlow SY8 2JU
www.pentabus-theatre.co.uk

Pilot Theatre
York Theatre Royal, St Leonard's Place, York YO1 7HD
www.pilot-theatre.com

Pursued by a Bear
Farnham Maltings, Bridge Square, Farnham GU9 7QR
www.pursuedbyabear.co.uk

Talawa Theatre Company
Plays that explore the Black British experience
3rd Floor, 23-25 Great Sutton Street, London EC1V 0DN
www.talawa.com

Tamasha Theatre Company
Plays that explore the Asian British experience
Unit 220 Great Guildford Business Square,
30 Great Guildford Street, London SE1 0HS
www.tamasha.org.uk

Tinderbox Theatre Company
Imperial Buildings, 72 High Street, Belfast BT1 2BE
www.tinderbox.org.uk

3. REGIONAL ORGANISATIONS THAT SUPPORT PLAYWRIGHTS

These regional organisations exist to develop the work of playwrights across the UK. Most of them have mailing lists for details of local events and opportunities, and some have script-reading services and operate writers' groups.

Menagerie (*East of England*)
www.menagerie.uk.com

New Writing North (*North East region*)
www.newwritingnorth.com

New Writing South (*South East region*)
www.newwritingsouth.com

North West Playwrights
www.newplaysnw.co.uk

Playwrights Studio Scotland
www.playwrightsstudio.co.uk

Script (*West Midlands*)
www.scriptonline.net

Script Yorkshire
www.scriptyorkshire.co.uk

Sgript Cymru – Contemporary Drama Wales
www.sgriptcymru.com

Soho Theatre and Writers Centre (*London*)
www.sohotheatre.com

South West Theatre Writing Network
c/o www.writernet.co.uk

Theatre Writing Partnership (*East Midlands*)
www.theatrewritingpartnership.org.uk

Tinderbox (*Northern Ireland*)
www.tinderbox.org.uk

4. LITERARY AGENCIES

Most of the major literary agencies representing playwrights are listed below.

If you're intending to seek representation, make sure you do some homework first. Find out who represents the playwrights you most admire, and try to identify the agents who are likely to find a connection with your work. Check the agency's website for any submission guidelines (some won't accept unsolicited scripts but may come to a performance or a reading instead).

The Agency
24 Pottery Lane, Holland Park, London W11 4LZ
Tel. 020 7727 1346
Fax. 020 7727 9037
info@theagency.co.uk
www.theagency.co.uk

Alan Brodie Representation Ltd
6th Floor, Fairgate House, 78 New Oxford Street,
London WC1A 1HB
Tel. 020 7079 7990
Fax. 020 7079 7999
info@alanbrodie.com
www.alanbrodie.com

Casarotto Ramsay and Associates Ltd
Waverley House, 7-12 Noel Street, London W1F 8GQ
Tel. 020 7287 4450
Fax. 020 7287 9128
info@casarotto.co.uk
www.casarotto.co.uk

Curtis Brown Group Ltd
Haymarket House, 28-29 Haymarket, London SW1Y 4SP
Tel. 020 7393 4400
Fax. 020 7393 4401
cb@curtisbrown.co.uk
www.curtisbrown.co.uk

Judy Daish Associates Ltd
2 St Charles Place, London W10 6EG
Tel. 020 8964 8811
Fax. 020 8964 8966
judy@judydaish.com

The Rod Hall Agency Ltd
6th Floor, Fairgate House, 78 New Oxford Street,
London WC1A 1HB
Tel. 020 7079 7987
Fax. 0845 638 4094
office@rodhallagency.com
www.rodhallagency.com

David Higham Associates
5-8 Lower John Street, Golden Square, London W1F 9HA
Tel. 020 7434 5900
Fax. 020 7437 1072
dha@davidhigham.co.uk
www.davidhigham.co.uk

ICM (International Creative Management)
Oxford House, 76 Oxford Street, London W1D 1BS
Tel. 020 7636 6565
Fax. 020 7323 0101
info@icmlondon.co.uk
www.icmlondon.co.uk

PFD (Peters Fraser & Dunlop)
Drury House, 34-43 Russell Street, London WC2B 5HA
Tel. 020 7344 1000
Fax. 020 7836 9541
postmaster@pfd.co.uk
www.pfd.co.uk

Micheline Steinberg Associates
104 Great Portland Street, London W1W 6PE
Tel. 020 7631 1310
Fax. 020 7631 1146
info@steinplays.com
www.steinplays.com

Julia Tyrrell Management
57 Greenham Road, London N10 1LN
Tel. 020 8374 0575
Fax. 020 8374 5580
julia@jtmanagement.co.uk
www.jtmanagement.co.uk

5. PLAY PUBLISHERS

These are the major UK publishers of new plays. They are unlikely to consider your play for publication unless it is going to be produced; check their websites for any submissions guidelines.

Faber and Faber
3 Queen Square, London WC1N 3AU
Tel. 020 7465 0045
Fax. 020 7465 0034
webmaster@faber.co.uk
www.faber.co.uk

Samuel French
52 Fitzroy Street, London W1T 5JR
Tel. 020 7387 9373
Fax. 020 7387 2161
www.samuelfrench-london.co.uk

Nick Hern Books
The Glasshouse, 49a Goldhawk Road, London W12 8QP
Tel. 020 8749 4953
Fax. 020 8735 0250
info@nickhernbooks.demon.co.uk
www.nickhernbooks.co.uk

Methuen Drama
(an imprint of **A&C Black**, which is a division of **Bloomsbury**)
A&C Black Publishers Ltd, 38 Soho Square, London W1D 3HB
Tel. 020 7758 0200
www.acblack.com

Oberon Books
521 Caledonian Road, London N7 9RH
Tel. 020 7607 3637
Fax. 020 7607 3629
oberon.books@btinternet.com
www.oberonbooks.com

Josef Weinberger Plays
12-14 Mortimer Street, London W1T 3JJ
Tel. 020 7580 2827
Fax. 020 7436 9616
general.info@jwmail.co.uk
www.josef-weinberger.com